leaf
Publishing

iPad

Ultimate Guide

Welcome

iPads are everywhere. You'll find them in people's backpacks, next to their beds, sitting on coffee tables.... you get the idea. To date, Apple has sold more than 425 million iPads. That means every single person in America could buy an iPad and there would still be more than 95 million to spare.

What I'm getting at, is that a lot of people know how to use the iPad. Most children know how to use an iPad. They understand it with an inherent nature that's almost baffling to many adults. Maybe it's because a touchscreen makes more logical sense than a keyboard or mouse. With a touchscreen, you can just reach out and touch whatever you want to interact with.

Of course, there's much more to iPad than just a touchscreen. It's possibly the most advanced piece of technology created by man, with components designed at the nanometre scale, and with software that can learn your routine, habits, and interests. That's what this book is all about. It's about revealing the features and abilities of the iPad, but in a concise, relatable way. You won't find any technical mumbo-jumbo, nor will it ramble on about features that most users don't need to know about. Instead, it will reveal the basics of the iPad, like what it's hardware does, how it's built-in apps work, and how you can use an iPad to enrich and improve your life.

Just before I go, if there's anything you would like to know that isn't covered in this book, feel free to send me an email at tom@leafpublishing.co.uk, and I'll be more than happy to help.

Tom Rudderham
Author
tom@leafpublishing.co.uk

Credits:

Author: Tom Rudderham
Editor: Zeljko Jurancevic
Copy Editor: Caroline Denham

Published by:
Leaf Publishing LTD
www.leafpublishing.co.uk

ISBN:
9798396685765

Contents

Welcome

The Basics

33
Learn about Multitasking

The Basics (continued)

Accessories

63
Discover trackpad gestures

Apps

69
Learn about the App Store

Web & Communication

90
Make a group
FaceTime call

Maps, Notes, & Utilities

115
Explore the
world in 3D

Camera & Photos

95
Learn how to take
panoramic photos

Entertainment & Fitness

Settings

141
Use Assistive
Touch

Terminology

Wondering what all those words and phrases mean?

The iPad is a state of the art piece of equipment, so perhaps it's inevitable that talking about it involves using a wide-ranging assortment of words, phrases, and terminology. In this book, you're going to hear a lot about the iPad hardware, software, and features. Don't worry, each one of them will be explained as we go, so you'll never feel confused or get lost halfway through a paragraph. To get you started, here are a few of the words we will be using constantly throughout this book...

Hardware

Whenever the word hardware is used, we're basically talking about the iPad in its physical form. The thing which you hold in your hand.

App

The word app is short for application. An application is a piece of software, separate from iPadOS, which lets you do something. There's an app on your iPad for taking a picture. There's an app for sending messages. There's an app for looking at your photos. I'm sure you get the idea.

Software

Think of software as a set of instructions for doing something on your iPad. These instructions might be millions of words long, and they were probably written by a large team of people. To most humans, it's utter gibberish. It looks something like this:

```
int main(int argc, char * argv[]) {
    @autoreleasepool {
        return UIApplicationMain( argc, argv, nil,
    NSStringFromClass( [AVCamAppDelegate
    class] ) );
    }
```

To a programmer who writes in Swift (Apple's programming language), this makes perfect sense. It's just a fraction of the code required to tell your iPad how to capture an image using its camera. The full piece of code is tens of thousands of lines long.

iOS

This is the name of the software which powers your iPad. It's one of the most complicated pieces of software ever created by man. It tells your iPad how to turn on, how to take a photo, how to browse the internet, how to scan your face when you want to unlock your iPad, plus so much more. It can also learn over time. iOS will learn about your habits, how you type to individual people, where you travel, what you look like and what you sound like. It uses all of this learning to help you type quicker, find photos quicker, and basically use your iPad in a more efficient manner.

You don't have to worry about security either, because all of this personal information is fully encrypted, and the really important stuff, like your voice and face information, never leaves your iPad.

When most people think of the word iOS, they imagine the home screen of their iPad. The place where all the icons are which let you open the internet browser or email application. You can think of it like that too, but really it's so much more.

Third-party apps

These are apps created by companies other than Apple. There are literally millions of them, and each app serves its own purpose. The most common apps you'll find include Facebook, Instagram, Amazon, and Netflix, but you can also find apps which let you add silly graphics onto photos, access your bank account, play games, and more. You'll find all of these apps in the...

App Store

Think of the App Store as a market for apps. Some apps are free, others cost a few dollars/pounds/euros. Some apps look like they are free, but ask for a payment to do something (this is called an "In-App Purchase"). You can find the App Store on your iPad. It has a bright blue icon with an abstract "A" in the middle.

Encryption

Think of encryption as a padlock for words, but instead of 0-9 on the padlock, it's A-Z, plus 0-9. The software on your iPad uses encryption all the time. Whenever you send a message to a friend, all the letters you type are scrambled up, sent to the other person, then de-scrambled on their device. The same goes for video calls you make using FaceTime, your credit cards details when you check out on the internet, and much more. Nearly everything you do on your iPad is encrypted, which is why even the FBI can't access your phone without your password or biometric information.

iCloud

Think of iCloud as a computer somewhere in the world where your photos, messages, apps, and settings are stored. Your iPad talks to this computer over the internet everyday to backup new photos, send new messages, and check for updates.

iPad

The most affordable iPad yet packed with every essential feature...

The iPad represents everything *classic* about the iPad. It sits in the sweet spot between size and weight, yet still has a large 10.9-inch display. It also happens to be the cheapest iPad you can buy.

There's a reason why the iPad is more affordable than it's larger and smaller siblings: it lacks a display with support for the P3 colour gamut (which makes photos and colours appear to really "pop" off the screen), and it also lacks support for True Tone (which alters the white balance of the display to match the environment around you). The screen is also non-laminated, which means it sits further behind the glass than other iPads. Internally, the iPad comes with the A14 Bionic processor, and it's limited to 2GB of RAM.

To most people, these slightly-lower specifications won't make much difference. Apps will take a fraction of a second longer to open, Safari tabs might refresh more often, and photographs will appear a little more faded, but for its price, the iPad represents an excellent purchase for anyone looking for a basic iPad.

Pros:

- Affordable.
- The "classic" iPad size.
- Full-size keyboard in landscape orientation.

Cons:

- Only supports the first-generation Apple Pencil.
- No face recognition.
- No ultra-wide camera.
- Two speakers, rather than four.
- The 10.3-inch display isn't as bright and colourful as other iPad displays.

iPad mini

It's almost handheld, but just as powerful...

A brand new design for the iPad mini introduces a larger edge-to-edge display, a blazingly fast processor, and four colours. It's basically an iPad Air shrunk down, with a beautiful Retina display, a Touch ID sensor in the power button, the A15 Bionic chipset, 3GB of memory, stereo speakers, and dual cameras. Even more surprising is that the iPad mini also supports the 1st generation Apple Pencil, so you can still sketch, draw, and make super accurate taps.

You might think that the iPad mini display features fewer pixels than its larger siblings, but you'd be wrong because the iPad mini manages to cram 3-million pixels into its 8.3-inch display. With support for the P3 colour gamut, an anti-reflective coating, plus 500 nits of brightness, the iPad mini display manages to look colourful, bright, and crisp wherever you are, even when you're outdoors in the sunshine.

The iPad mini is just an amazing tablet that can be held comfortably in one hand, and it slips into a rucksack or purse without adding any considerable weight. It's a tablet which you can leave lying around the house, yet it doesn't take up any space.

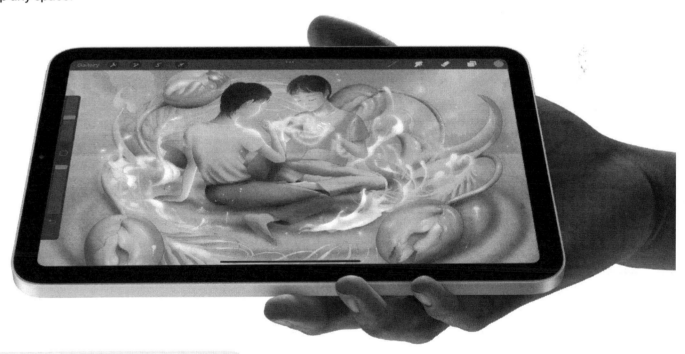

Pros:
- Very comfortable to hold.
- Small and light makes it easier to carry.
- Affordable.
- A large 8.3-inch display.

Cons:
- Only supports the first-generation Apple Pencil.
- No face recognition.
- No ultra-wide camera.
- Two speakers, rather than four.
- The small screen makes multitasking and productivity apps difficult to use.

iPad Air

Featuring a beautiful display and powerful processor...

The iPad Air pretty much is an iPad Pro; well, the 10.5-inch 2017 iPad Pro. It looks almost the same, it's packed with some seriously fast hardware, it supports the same Smart Keyboard, and it also works with the Apple Pencil (albeit the first-generation Apple Pencil). Think of the iPad Air as the previous-generation iPad Pro, at a much-reduced price.

Let's talk about specifications for a moment, because packed within the iPad Air is one of Apple's most powerful mobile CPUs: the Apple M1 chip. That's the same chip included in Apple's mainstream desktop and laptop computers, meaning the iPad Air is incredibly fast, and capable of rendering web pages in an instant. It also supports the ability to run multiple apps at once - a feature that we cover later in this book.

So who is the iPad Air aimed at? It's not aimed at professionals, because they're far more likely to be tempted by the latest iPad Pro; and it's not aimed at those who want a tiny tablet to carry around, because the iPad mini covers that segment. Instead, the iPad Air is aimed at those who just want a really good iPad. An iPad which covers all of the classic iPad stuff (like gaming, watching movies, and browsing the web), but which also supports an excellent typing experience thanks to support for the Smart Keyboard.

Pros:
- Similar specs to the iPad Pro, but considerably cheaper.
- Large 10.5-inch display.
- Incredibly fast, and able to run multiple apps at once.
- Touch ID is convenient for those wearing a face mask.

Cons:
- No face recognition.
- No ultra-wide camera.
- Two speakers, rather than four.

iPad Pro

A powerful and versatile tablet with a massive screen...

An entirely new camera system, faster internals, and double the storage make the latest iPad Pro a powerful alternative to traditional desktop computing.

Sit the iPad Pro next to an iPad Air, and you might struggle to tell them apart. Both feature a screen that stretches from edge to edge, and both have a beautiful aluminium frame, but there are some subtle differences. The iPad Pro features the Apple M2 chip, which delivers up to 15 per cent faster performance alongside a GPU that provides up to 35 per cent faster graphics performance. It also has a Face ID sensor - the same sensor included with the iPhone - which enables you to unlock the iPad using just your face. The screen comes in two sizes, both of which are larger at either 11-inch or 12.9-inch. Those screens are also twice as fast as the iPad Air's, able to refresh at 120 times per second, rather than 60, which means things slide across the screen more smoothly, and it's ever so slightly more responsive to the touch.

Over on the back, the iPad Pro features a 2x camera lens, so you can take photos and videos of things further away, plus a LIDAR lens for enhancing AR apps. Around the sides, it has four speakers for more immersive sound, and it also supports the second-generation Apple Pencil, which charges magnetically and snaps to the side of your iPad.

While these differences are subtle, they all add up to make the iPad Pro a compelling device. One that can replace a laptop for many users while also enhancing creativity for those who can take advantage of the Apple Pencil.

Pros:

- Massive 12.9-inch display makes drawing and working with productivity apps easy.
- Beautiful display that reaches to the edge of the device.
- Can replace a laptop computer.
- Supports latest Apple Pencil, plus the Magic Keyboard.
- AR sensor on the back future-proofs the iPad Pro.

Cons:

- 12.9-inch iPad is heavy, especially with the Magic Keyboard case.
- Expensive.

Still wondering which iPad to get?

Some helpful tips for deciding whether to go regular, Air, mini, or Pro...

If the last few pages didn't help, then here are some examples of how each model of iPad suits different lifestyles and choices...

"All I need is the basics"

If you just want to check emails, browse the web, and look at Facebook, then the 10th generation iPad is the choice for you. Now all you need to do is pick a colour. You can choose from blue, pink, silver, or yellow.

"I want the smallest iPad"

The iPad mini is the perfect portable tablet. With its 8.3-inch display, it's small enough to be held in one hand, yet it still supports every iPad app, and the Apple Pencil.

"I'm pretty creative and/or productive"

If you're planning on sketching, painting, working with 3D models, or doing anything else creative, then the iPad Pro is your best choice. It has the fastest processor, which is essential for rendering 3D models, and it has the quickest screen refresh rate, which makes drawing and modelling super smooth.

"I want to play games and watch a lot of movies"

With its large 12.9-inch display, the iPad Pro is the best choice for both gaming and media consumption. The bigger screen makes watching high-definition video content more immersive, while also making it easier to control games.

"I m on a budget, and just want an iPad"

If you just want to check emails, browse the web, and look at Facebook, then the 9th generation iPad is the choice for you. Now all you need to do is pick a colour. You can choose from silver or space grey.

The iPad buttons

A quick overview of what each physical button does...

Unbox your iPad for the first time and you'll likely marvel at its machine-polished aluminium body and large glass screen. Then you'll notice the physical buttons which run along the edges. They're not labelled, so if you've never used an iPad before than it's not clear what each button does. Here's an overview of each button alongside the many holes and sockets scattered around the device...

iPad (10th gen) iPad Pro, iPad Air, & iPad mini:

Power Button

When off:

- Press and hold to turn your iPad on. On the regular iPad and iPad Air, this also acts as a fingerprint sensor to unlock the device.

When on:

- Press it once to lock your iPad.
- Press and hold along with a volume button to turn off your iPad.
- Press and hold to enable Siri.
- Press it twice to access Apple Pay.

Volume Up

- Press once to turn the volume up.
- Press and hold to quickly turn the volume up.
- Press while using the Camera app to take a photo.
- Press simultaneously with the Power button to take a screenshot.

Volume Down

- Press once to turn the volume down.
- Press and hold to quickly mute the audio.
- Press while using the Camera app to take a photo.

iPad (9th gen):

Power Button

When off:
- Press and hold to turn your iPad on.

When on:
- Press it once to lock your iPad.
- Press and hold to turn off your iPad.

Volume Up
- Press once to turn the volume up.
- Press and hold to quickly turn the volume up.
- Press while using the Camera app to take a photo.
- Press simultaneously with the Home button to take a screenshot.

Volume Down
- Press once to turn the volume down.
- Press and hold to quickly mute the audio.
- Press while using the Camera app to take a photo.

Home Button
- Return to the Home screen.
- Press and hold to enable Siri.
- Press it twice while locked to access Apple Pay.
- Press it twice while unlocked to open the Multitasking screen.

Setup and activate your iPad

Discover how to activate your brand new iPad...

So you've bought a brand new iPad, and you've unwrapped it from the box. The next step is to activate it for the very first time. This process will let you choose a language to use, set your location and local time, and activate key features such as Siri (a helpful voice-activated assistant). Once your iPad is activated, you'll be able to use it to browse the web, send messages, plus much more.

How to activate an eSIM

1 If you have a QR code from your cellular provider, open the Camera app, point it at the QR code, and then tap the yellow button which appears on-screen.

2 Follow the on-screen instructions to activate and add your eSIM.

3 If you don't have a QR code, open the **Settings** app, select **Cellular Data or Mobile Data**, then tap **Add eSIM**. Next, follow the on-screen instructions to activate your eSIM.

4 If your eSIM is not activated during the setup process, then open the **Settings** app, tap **Cellular Data or Mobile Data**, select your eSIM plan, then tap **Turn on this line**.

How to insert a SIM card (iPad with cellular only)

1 Look in the iPad box for the SIM tray tool. It's thin, silver, and looks like a paperclip.

2 Insert the pointy end of the SIM tray tool into the small hole on the right-side of your iPad.

3 Press hard, and the sim tray will pop out slightly.

4 Use your fingernail to pull the sim tray out, then carefully place your SIM card into it. You might have to flip it around to make sure it fits properly.

5 Slide the SIM tray back into your iPad and you're good to go.

Activate your iPad

1 Start by turning on your iPad for the first time. To do this, just press the **power** button on the upper-right side. After a moment or two the Apple logo will appear.

2 When the Hello screen appears, **swipe up** from the bottom of the screen to continue.

3 Tap the language you want to use for your iPad, then tap the country or region.

Use the Quick Start tool to copy across your old iPad

If you're going from an old iPad to a new one, then you can use the Quick Start tool to automatically copy across all of your messages, photos, apps, settings, and personal data to the new iPad. It works quickly and it's easy to do...

1 Place your new iPad next to your old one. The Quick Start screen will automatically offer the option of using your Apple ID to set up the new device. Make sure it's the right Apple ID, then tap **Continue**.

2 Wait for an animation to appear on your new iPad, then use the camera viewfinder on the old iPad and centre the animation in the middle of the screen. When you see a button that says **Finish on New [Device]**, tap the button and follow the on-screen options to transfer your apps, data, and settings to the new device.

Use the Quick Start tool to copy your data from iCloud

If you don't have your old iPad to hand, then you can sync all of your messages, apps, accounts, and other personal data using iCloud, which works over the internet. To do this:

1 After activating your iPad, tap **Restore from iCloud Backup**.

2 Sign into iCloud using your Apple ID and password.

3 Choose the most recent backup. You can check by looking at the date and size of each backup.

4 If you've purchased apps and iTunes content using multiple Apple IDs, then you'll be asked for the passwords to each one.

5 Wait for the process to finish. This may take some time, so it's a good idea to keep your device connected to Wi-Fi and a power source.

6 After the process has completed your iPad will turn on and activate, but it will still need to download content such as apps and photos, so be patient as it restores all of your data.

Touch ID

Setup Touch ID so you can unlock your iPad using your fingerprint...

A fingerprint is one of the most secure methods of locking your iPad, because afterall, the chances of someone else with the same fingerprint coming across your iPad is pretty small. Using your fingerprint to unlock your iPad is also pretty efficient, because it takes less than a second for your iPad to read your print and unlock the device.

Keeping your personal data safe is one of Apple's most pressing priorities, so here's what the company does to ensure your fingerprint never leaves your iPad:

● The iPad and its operating system can never access your fingerprint data. Only the fingerprint sensor beneath the Home button can access your print, and it only sends a yes or no signal to the operating system when you place your fingertip on the sensor.

● Your fingerprint never leaves the physical device. That means it can't be accessed by the NSA, hackers or anyone else.

Set up Touch ID

Your iPad will ask you to set up Touch ID when you activate it for the very first time. If you skipped that step, just open the **Settings** app, select **Touch & Passcode** then tap **Add a Fingerprint.**

Place your thumb or finger on the **Home** button. You'll see a graphic of a fingerprint appear and start to turn red. Keep placing your fingerprint on the Home button until the graphic has completely filled.

You'll then be asked to repeat the process, but this time to place the edges of your finger on the Home button. Once you've finished, tap **Continue.**

Place Your Finger

Lift and rest your finger on the Home button repeatedly.

Give each fingerprint a name

If you're adding multiple fingerprints, then it's a good idea to give them names. This helps you to manage the prints of multiple people, or work out which ones to delete at a later time. To do this, go to **Settings** > **Touch & Passcode,** then tap on the fingerprint you wish to name.

How to delete a fingerprint

To remove a fingerprint, go to **Settings** > **Touch & Passcode,** then tap on the fingerprint you wish to delete. Next, tap the red **Delete Fingerprint** text.

Face ID

Setup Face ID so you can unlock your iPad Pro using your face...

If you own an iPad Pro then you've might have noticed that it doesn't have a Home button or fingerprint sensor. Instead, a small array of sensors above the screen scan your face, then automatically unlock your iPad Pro in the blink of an eye. It's a feature called Face ID, and it's way more advanced than you might think.

It works by using a TrueDepth Camera System to recognise you. Basically, an infrared camera can see your face, even in the dark, while a dot projector maps your face with more than 30,000 dots. All of this data is used to create a mathematical model of your face. This mathematical model is used to prevent people from using photos of you to unlock your iPad. Face ID also looks for telltale signs of life (like moving or blinking eyes), to know that a model of your face wasn't used. Once it has confirmed all of this (which usually takes less than a second) then Face ID tells your iPad that it's definitely you; and that things are good to go.

Set up Face ID

Your iPad will ask you to set up Face ID when you activate it for the very first time. If you skipped that step, just open the **Settings** app, select **Face ID & Passcode** then tap **Enrol Face.**

Follow the on-screen instructions to add your face. You'll be asked to gently move your head in a circular motion. That's because Face ID performs best when all angles of your face are captured. Once the process is complete, tap **Done** to enrol your face.

Create an alternative look

If you sometimes change your look in a drastic way (for example via makeup, with a wig, or with extensive accessories), then you can teach Face ID to recognise you with these changes. To do this, get ready with your alternative look, then go to **Settings > Face ID & Passcode**, then tap **Set Up an Alternate Appearance**.

The Lock Screen

Use gestures to unlock your iPad, open the camera, and more...

Press either the **Home** or **Power** buttons on your iPad and the Lock Screen will quickly fade into view. If you've received any notifications, such as a text message or a news story, then you'll see them in the middle of the screen. Otherwise, you'll just see the background wallpaper, time, and date.

1 Swipe down from the top-right corner to access Control Centre.

2 Tap a notification to find out more, or swipe it to the left to manage any further notifications.

3 Swipe from the left to access Spotlight, where all your widgets, shortcuts and Spotlight search can be found.

4 Swipe from the right to open the Camera app.

5 If using an iPad Pro or Air, swipe up from the bottom of the screen to go to the Home Screen. If using an iPad or iPad mini, press the **Home** button to unlock your iPad and go to the Home Screen.

The Home Screen

Discover how to interact with apps and folders...

From the Lock screen, swipe upwards from the bottom of the screen and your iPad will unlock and display the Home screen. If you're using a traditional iPad then you can also press the Home button. You'll see multiple icons across the screen. These represent the apps installed on your iPad. To open one of these apps just tap on its icon. To close the app and go back to the Home screen, just swipe upwards from the bottom of the screen. You can also access the Dock at any time, even when you're in an app, by swiping up from the bottom of the screen by just a small amount.

1. • Tap and hold on an app icon to see a secondary menu.
   • Tap and hold on an app icon for three seconds to move, re-arrange, or delete apps.

2. To make a folder of apps, tap and hold on an app icon, wait for it to start jiggling, then drag the app on top of another.

3. Swipe left or right across an empty part of the screen to see more apps.

4. This is the Dock. You can put important apps here and you'll always find them at the bottom of the Home Screen.

Gestures and buttons

Learn about key gestures used for controlling your iPad...

The vast, high-definition screen that spreads out across your iPad is a technological marvel. You might not know it, but it actually supports up to 10 individual fingertips, and works by detecting the static charge on your skin — not heat or pressure as many often believe. By tapping and gesturing on the screen you can take full advantage of everything iOS has to offer, such as zooming into content, rotating images and more.

Additionally, the hardware buttons on your iPad enable you to activate Siri or shut the entire thing off. Many of these functions are entirely intuitive, but for those who have never interacted with an iPad before, let's go over them...

Return to the Home screen

Whenever you're in an app, swipe up quickly from the very bottom of the screen to return to the Home screen. On an older iPad, then you can also press the **Home** button.

Access the Dock

The Dock is where your favourite apps and most recently used apps are located. You'll see the Dock at the bottom of the Home screen, but you can also access it whenever you're in an app by swiping up from the bottom of the screen then stopping after an inch or two.

Access the multitasking screen

Swipe up from the bottom of the screen then stop halfway to see all the apps you've recently opened. If using an older iPad, then you can also press the **Home** button twice.

Force quit an app

While you're viewing the multitasking screen, push an app thumbnail upwards and off the screen to force quit it. You only need to do this if an app has crashed and stopped working.

Power off

If you'd like to fully turn off your iPad, then hold down both the **power** button and **volume up** buttons. On an older iPad, you only need to hold down the **power** button.

Jump between apps

Want to quickly jump between apps? Swipe along the very bottom of the screen, left-to-right, and you'll jump between apps.

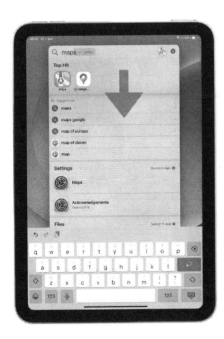

Access Search

From the Home screen, pull the screen down using your finger to access the Search screen. From here you can search for apps, emails, contacts and more.

Swipe to go back

To go back a panel or page, swipe from the left-side of the screen inwards. This works great in apps like Safari, Mail, or Settings.

Access Siri

To talk to Siri, press and hold the **power** button. You can also say "*Hey Siri*" out-loud to enable Siri. If you're using an older iPad, press and hold the **Home** button instead.

How to use Control Centre

Discover how to quickly toggle controls...

Tucked above the screen are a helpful set of buttons for toggling settings and activating features. They include a slider for controlling the screen brightness, a button for enabling Wi-Fi, shortcuts to toggle Airplane Mode, Night Shift mode and more. To access these shortcuts at any time swipe down from the top-right corner of the screen.

You can long-press on any of these buttons to access further settings or controls that are easier to use. To close Control Centre swipe back up or tap in the empty space below Control Centre.

1. These four buttons enable you to toggle Airplane mode, your cellular connection, Wi-Fi, and Bluetooth. Tap and hold on this box and you can also access controls for AirDrop and Personal Hotspot.

2. This box in the upper-right corner lets you control audio playback. If you have wireless headphones connected then you can connect to them using the AirPlay button in the very top corner of this box.

3. If you don't want the screen to rotate into landscape/portrait mode whenever you rotate your iPad, then tap the **Orientation Lock** button.

4. Tap on **Focus** to quickly enable Do Not Disturb, or to choose from a number of custom notification modes where you can specify who can get in touch, which apps can notify you, and even choose which apps appear on the Home Screen. Turn to page **31** to find out more.

5. These sliders enable you to adjust the screen brightness and audio volume. You can tap and hold on each one to make it bigger and easier to use.

6. Tap the **Torch** icon to instantly turn on the flash at the back of your iPad. You can also tap and hold to choose between bright, medium and low settings.

7. Tap the **Timer** or **Camera** buttons to instantly open these apps. You can also add additional shortcusts to features such as accessibility shortcuts, screen recording mode and more (see below).

Customise Control Centre

If you want to add additional buttons to Control Centre, or remove those that you don't use very often, simply open the **Settings** app and tap **Control Centre.** On the following panel you'll find shortcuts to add and remove options. You can also rearrange the options by using the drag buttons to customise Control Centre to your exact needs.

Search your iPad

Search your iPad for apps and content...

If you're looking for something specific on your iPad, such as a particular app or settings, then the search panel is often a good place to start. It can find nearly anything on your iPad, including content inside of apps. It can also search the web and make helpful suggestions.

How to access search

There are two ways to access the search screen:

1 From the Home screen, swipe down from the middle of the screen and the search panel will appear. You can use this panel to look for messages, songs, notes, and even search for things on the web.

2 If you have a keyboard attached to your iPad, then hold the **Command** key and press the **spacebar** to access search. This works anywhere on your iPad, even when you're using an app.

Hide apps and app content from appearing in search results

You can adjust the search panel to hide individual apps and results while you're searching. To do this:

1 Go to **Settings** > **Siri & Search**.

2 Scroll down then select an app.

3 Untoggle **Show App in Search**, and **Suggest Content in Search** to prevent results and shortcut suggestions from appearing.

Widgets

Add additional information to the Home Screen...

Think of widgets as small windows of helpful information that you can place around the Home Screen of your iPad. You'll find widgets that display the latest news, widgets that display photos from your library, and even a "smart" widget, which changes throughout the day to show you helpful information.

How to browse and add widgets

To browse the widget library, go to the Home Screen of your iPad, then **tap and hold** on an empty space. When you see the app icons start to wiggle, tap the **plus (+)** button in the top-left corner.

The first widget you'll see is a suggested list based on your recent activity. Down the side bar is a of every widget available. If you already know which widget you're looking for, then you can also use the search field at the top of the window to find it.

Tap on a widget within the list, and you'll see the various sizes it's available in. Some take up the space of four app icons, some six, while a few (such as Music) can be as big as sixteen app icons.

Example widget layouts:

Rearrange widgets

If you're unhappy with the placement of widgets, then **tap and hold** on a widget until it starts to wiggle. Next, slide the widget around the screen using your finger. Once you've moved the widget to a suitable place, tap the **Done** button in the top-right corner.

Stack widgets

You can drag and drop one widget on top of another, and so long as they are both the same size, they will stack on top of each other. This means you can swipe vertically across the widget to go from one to another.

Adjust smart widgets

The Smart Stack widget will change depending on the time of day and what you're doing, so sometimes you might see the latest news, or another time your recent photos. To prevent Smart Stack from automatically suggesting new content, tap and hold on it until it starts to wiggle, then tap on it. In the pop-up window, you can toggle Smart Rotate and Widget Suggestions on or off by using the blue buttons below the widget.

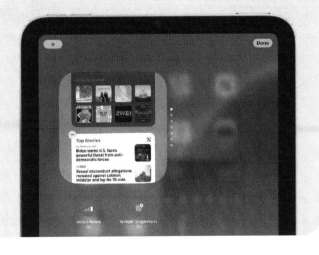

Widget notes:

- You can have a Home Screen filled entirely with widgets.

- You can also have a Home Screen with just a single widget on it, and nothing else.

- Widgets can only be placed directly next to apps, so you can't have a widget at the bottom of the screen with empty space above it.

- Widgets on the Home Screen work like apps, so when you're ready to remove one, **tap and hold** on it, wait a moment, then tap the **minus (-)** button which appears.

Display settings

Learn how to adjust the display to meet your needs...

The display of your iPad is its most crucial component because it's the one you spend the most time prodding, poking, and looking at.

You might not know it, but there are some essential settings available for the iPad which let you adjust the screen to suit your needs better. You can play around with the brightness, disable Night Shift, and capture what's on the screen to share with others...

Adjust the brightness

If you'd like to adjust the brightness of the display, just swipe down from the top-right corner of the screen to access Control Centre, then slide the **brightness** slider up or down. You can **tap and hold** on this slider to make it bigger and easier to use.

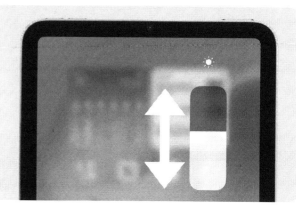

Disable True Tone

True Tone is a clever feature that adjusts the colour tone of the display to match the environment around you. So if you're sitting in a room with yellowish light, the screen will subtly change to suit the environment.

If you prefer the screen to always look pure white, open the **Settings** app and go to **Display & Brightness,** then toggle **True Tone** off. You can also disable True Tone from Control Centre. Just tap and hold on the brightness slider, then tap the **True Tone** button.

Disable Auto-Brightness

By default your iPad will automatically adjust the brightness of the display to match the conditions of your environment; so if you're in a dark room, the screen will dim, while under direct sunlight it will set to maximum brightness.

To turn this off or on, go to **Settings** > **Accessibility** > **Display & Text Size** and turn **Auto-Brightness** off.

Take a screenshot

If you want to share something interesting on your screen, then taking a screenshot of it is a great way to do this. Here's how it works:

1 Press the **Power** button and **Volume Up** buttons at the same time to capture the screen. On an original iPad, press the **Home** button and **Power** buttons at the same time.

2 You'll see a thumbnail of the screenshot minimise and snap to the bottom left corner.

3 Leave the thumbnail alone for a few seconds and it will automatically be saved to the Photos app. You can also swipe the thumbnail to the left to quickly save it.

4 Tap the **pencil** button in the upper-right corner to annotate the screenshot, crop it, share it, or delete it.

Create a video recording of the screen

1 Start by adding the Screen Recording widget to Control Centre. To do this go to **Settings > Control Centre**, scroll down then tap the **plus (+)** button next to **Screen Recording**.

2 When you're ready to capture the screen, open Control Centre, then tap the **Screen Recording** button (it looks like the outline of a circle with a dot in the middle). After three seconds the recording will begin.

3 Tap the **red bar** at the top of the screen to stop the recording.

4 To capture audio, tap and hold on the **Screen Recording** button within Control Centre, then tap **Microphone**.

How to manage Notifications

Discover how to manage notifications...

However you use your iPad, you're going to receive notifications on a regular basis. Notifications usually appear when you have a new message, or if an app wants to get your attention. If your iPad is locked, then the notification will appear as a bubble on the Lock Screen. If you're using your device when the notification arrives, then it will appear as a floating panel at the top of the screen. If an app wants to get your attention, then you might see a red dot above its icon on the Home screen.

If there's one annoying aspect about receiving notifications on an iPad, it's that you can't simply ignore them. Try to do that, and they'll only end up in the Notification Centre, forever awaiting an action from yourself. Similarly, if you try and ignore that little red dot above an app icon, and it'll never go away. Thankfully, you can customise, hide, and even disable notifications from individual apps...

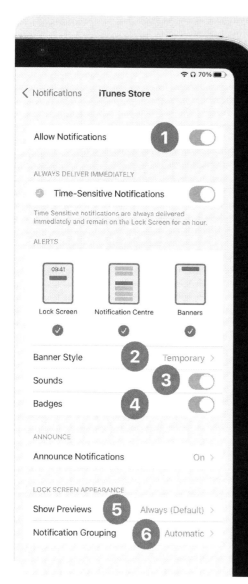

Customise notifications

To customise how apps notifiy you, go to **Settings > Notifications**, then select an app. On the following panel you'll see these options:

1. **Allow Notifications:** Toggle on to receive notifications from the app you selected.

2. **Banners:** Choose how you want notifications to appear when your iPad is unlocked. Tap **Temporary** to display alerts for a short period of time, or tap **Persistent** to have alerts stay on the screen until you act on it.

3. **Sounds:** Toggle audio alerts for when you receive a notification. Some apps, such as Messages, let you pick a custom sound too.

4. **Badges:** These appears as numbered red circles above an app icon. Uncheck this button to prevent badges from appearing over a specific app.

5. **Show Previews:** Choose what you want to see when you get a notification, like a text message.

6. **Notification Grouping.** Tap on this option to decide how multiple notifications from a single app appear on the Lock Screen.

Clear all notifications

If you have a stack of notifications waiting for you in Notification Centre, then you can clear them all at once by tapping and holding on the small **X** button, then **Clear**.

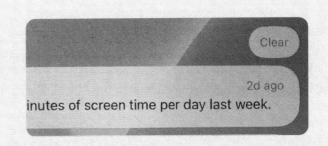

Interact with notifications

If a notification appears while you're using your iPad, pull it down from the top of the screen using your finger to interact with it. For example, if you get a message, pull the notification down and you'll be able to send a reply without going into the Messages app.

Manage notifications

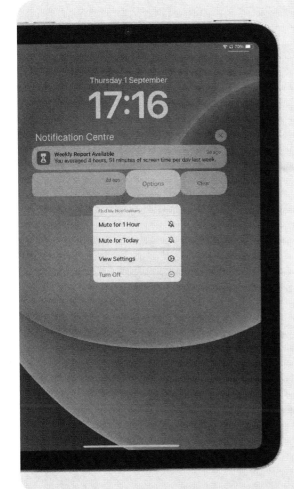

If you receive an unwanted notification from an app or person, then you can customise how any further notifications from this source will appear. To do this, **swipe the notification to the left** then tap the **Options** button. A number of options will then appear:

- **Mute for 1 Hour**
  Turn off any further notifications from this app for the next hour.

- **Mute for Today**
  Similar to above, but with this option you can mute any further notifications for the rest of the day.

- **View Settings**
  Jump to the apps notifications settings panel (see back across page for more details).

- **Turn Off**
  Tap this to disable any further notifications from this app. To re-enable notifications for the app, go to **Settings > Notifications > [app name]**, then toggle **Allow Notifications** on.

Use Focus mode to prevent distractions

Block unnecessary distractions and notifications while you're at work, home, or exercising...

Using Focus mode, you can set an activity that you're doing - such as working, exercising, or relaxing at home - and then block any notifications, apps, and even people that are unrelated to those tasks. You can ask Focus to automatically enable at fixed times, when you arrive or leave a location, or when you open an app. You can even hide individual pages on the Home Screen.

When set up correctly, Focus mode is a powerful way to help you concentrate on what's important at any given time or place. It means you can set up a Work mode that shows all your work-related apps, while also blocking notifications from friends and family; then at the end of the day, automatically use a Home mode to show your social media apps while blocking any notifications from the office. Here's how it works:

Set up a Personal Focus mode

Start by opening the **Settings** app, then tap **Focus**. You'll find several pre-made options like Do Not Disturb, Books, and Driving. Below are two options called Personal and Sleep, which are waiting for you to customise. Let's select **Personal**, and explore how Focus mode works in more detail...

1 Add contacts

After selecting **Personal**, tap **Next** on the welcome screen, then select anyone from your Contacts book that you would like to be able to reach you while Personal mode is active. Focus mode will make some suggestions based on people you regularly contact, but you can add more by tapping **Add**. Tap **Allow** when you're ready to continue.

2 Add apps and finish

You can now select which apps can send notifications to you while Personal mode is active. Again, you can add more by tapping **Add**. Tap **Allow** when you're ready to continue, then **Done** to finish setting up Personal Mode. You have now created a Focus mode which only lets certain people and apps get in touch when activated.

Set a Focus schedule

Let's add a schedule to a Focus mode, so that it automatically kicks in at 5 PM, then turns off at midnight.

To begin, select any Focus mode, then tap **Add Schedule**. On the following panel, choose **Time**, then use the **From** and **To** buttons to select 17:00 and 00:00. You can also choose which days of the week Personal mode automatically activates by selecting and unselecting the REPEAT buttons at the bottom of the panel.

Automatically enable Focus mode at a location

If you want to set a Focus mode to automatically enable when you reach a location (such as home, the office, or the gym), then select a Focus mode, then tap **Add Schedule**. On the following panel, tap **Location**, then enter a place or address using the search field near the top of the screen. Once found, you can adjust the radius of the area where the Focus mode engages by using the map slider at the bottom of the screen. Tap **Done** when you're ready to save your changes.

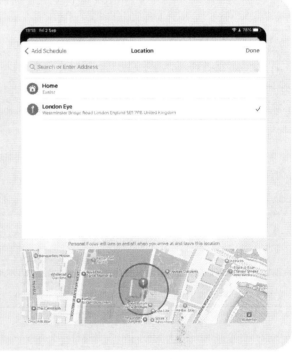

Choose which Home Page/s to show

To help you further concentrate while Focus mode is enabled, you can show and hide entire pages of apps on the Home Screen.

To do this, select a Focus mode, look for the CUSTOMISE SCREENS panel, then tap Choose. On the next panel, tick the pages you wish to show when Focus mode is enabled. Tap **Done** to save your changes.

How to multitask

Use two apps at once, or watch a video while doing something else...

With the iPad, multitasking between two apps is a useful and realistic way to work. That's because of the sheer size of the iPad display, which makes it possible to run two full-sized apps at once, watch a video stream while browsing the web, or quickly check your emails while looking through photos. You can also access the Dock at any time, letting you quickly jump between your favourite apps.

There are three multitasking modes included with the iPad:

- Slide Over lets you quickly open a second app without leaving the one you're currently using.

- Split View enables you to run two apps at the same time.

- Picture in Picture lets you watch a video while still doing other things.

Let's take a look at all the multitasking features in a little more detail...

Quickly access the Dock

The Dock contains all of your favourite apps. You can always find it at the bottom of the Home screen. You can also access it when you're using an app by swiping up from the bottom of the screen then stopping after an inch or two. To close the Dock swipe it back down or tap in the space above it.

The Dock is split into two parts. On the left side are your favourite apps. You can add up to 8 apps at a time. To do this just visit the Home screen, tap and hold on an app then drag it onto the Dock. On the right side of the Dock are your three most recently opened apps, plus a button for accessing the App Library, where you can browse and explore every app on your iPad.

Run two apps at the same time using Split View

With Split View you can run two apps at the same time. This means you can browse the web while making notes, chat with a friend while looking through photos... the options are endless. Here's how it works:

1 Open the first app, then tap the **options** button at the very top of the screen. It looks like this:

2 A small control panel will then appear with three options:

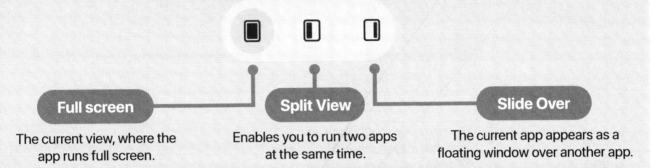

Full screen
The current view, where the app runs full screen.

Split View
Enables you to run two apps at the same time.

Slide Over
The current app appears as a floating window over another app.

3 Choose the **Split View** option. The Home Screen will then appear, enabling you to choose which app takes up the other half of the screen. To make a choice, tap on an app, and it will then appear side-by-side alongside the first app:

Split View notes:

● While in Split View, you can resize apps by dragging the black bar from left to right.

● To replace one app with another, open the Dock by swiping up the screen, then drag an app from the Dock and slide it over the app you wish to replace.

● To close Split View, drag the black bar that separates the two apps off the screen.

Use Slide Over to control music

With Slide Over view, you can call up a small, windowed view of an app (such as the Music app), and control both apps simultaneously:

1 Open the first app then slide your finger upwards from the bottom of the screen to access the Dock.

2 Drag the second app you wish to use from the Dock, and slide it towards the left or right side of the screen.

3 Let go of your finger and the app will hover in place. Slide View is now enabled.

To move a Slide Over app around the screen, place your finger on the top middle part of the app (where you see a grey line), then slide the app to its new position.

To snap a Slide Over app into place, so it can be run in Split View, tap the multitasking button at the top of the window, then choose whether to snap the app to the left or right side of the screen.

To dismiss a Slide Over app, simply slide it off the screen to the left or right. The app will still be there, even when you can't see it. You can bring it back by sliding your finger inwards from the side of the screen.

Use drag and drop to move things between apps

Drag and drop is a truly powerful tool on iPad, and it's simple to use. It works by letting you drag anything from one app to another. It can be an image, a link, a chunk of text... whatever you like. You can even drag multiple items at once to save time. It takes a little practice, but once perfected you'll wonder how you ever lived without this clever feature.

1 Let's start by running the Photos app and Notes app in either Split view. In the Photos app, tap and hold on a photo. After a moment it will lift off the screen and attach to your finger.

2 Next, slide the photo over to the Notes app. You'll see a small green icon appear when drag and drop is available. Once you see this let go. The photo will now be dropped into place. It's that simple!

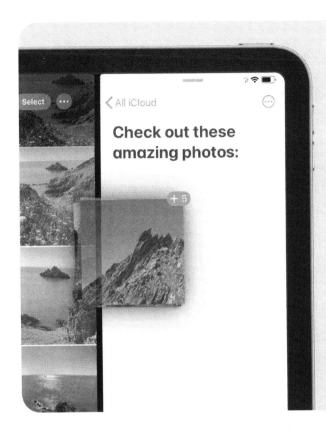

How to drag and drop multiple items

While we're still looking at the Photos and Notes app...

1 **Tap and hold** on a photo, then wait for it to attach to your finger.

2 Tap on another photo and it will also attach to your finger (you might need to use two fingers to do this).

3 You can select as many photos as you wish using this technique.

4 Slide the photos over the Notes app and let go. They will all drop into place!

Drag and drop files into other apps

It's possible to drag items into another app that's not in Split or Slideover view. In fact, there are multiple ways you can drag items to another app. Begin by selecting an item (or multiple items), then:

- While tapping and holding on an item, return to the home screen with your other hand, open the app you wish to move the items to, then drop them into place.

- Use your other hand to swipe up from the bottom of the screen to enable the Dock, select the app then drop the item/s in place.

- Use four fingers and swipe across the screen to go between earlier apps. When you get to the right app, drop the item/s in place.

Use Stage Manager to run multiple apps at once

If you own an iPad Air or iPad Pro released after mid-2021, then it's possible to use Stage Manager, which takes multitasking to a whole new level.

Typically, when you open an app on your iPad, you see it running full screen. With Stage Manager activated, you can resize apps so they take up less than the whole screen, then open another app and run it side-by-side. It's similar to how a traditional computer or laptop works, with multiple windows open at once. Here's how it looks in action:

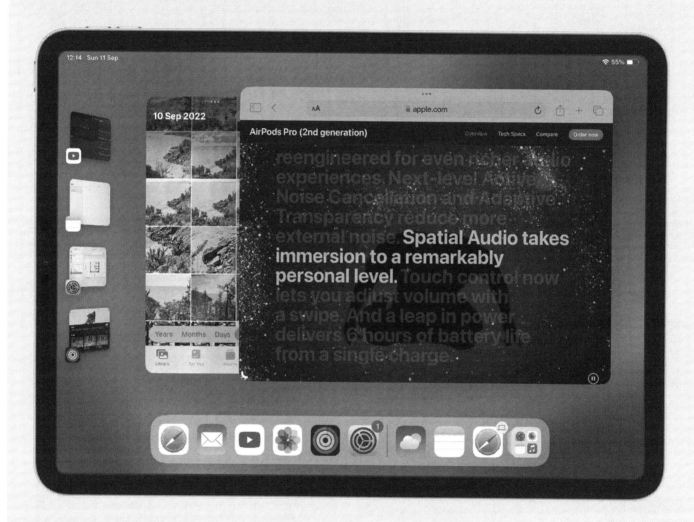

How to activate Stage Manager

Stage Manager needs to be turned on in the Settings app before you can use it. To do this, open the **Settings** app, select **Home Screen & Multitasking**, tap on **Stage Manager**, and then toggle it on.

Next, look in the bottom-right corner and you'll see a curved line. This enables you to re-size the Settings app window. To do this, tap and hold on the curved line and then drag it inwards towards the centre of the screen. You'll see the Settings app become smaller. Once you're happy with a window size, let go, and you'll be running Stage Manager mode.

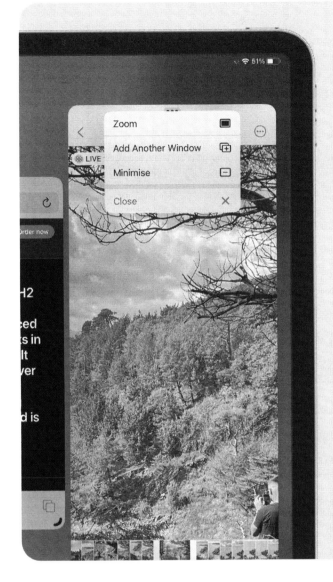

Manage multiple apps with Stage Manager

To use more than one app simultaneously at a time:

1 Open the first app you wish to run.

2 Next, drag and drop the second app from either the Recent Apps section or the Dock, onto the main screen.

3 Your apps are now running side-by-side. You can keep adding apps using this process and resize them as you see fit.

4 To rearrange an app, tap and hold on the top of the app, then drag it to a new location. If you drag it on top of another app, then it will move to the front.

5 To make an app bigger or smaller, tap and hold on the **curved line**, then drag the corner of the app to create a new size.

6 To remove an app from Stage Manager, either drag it back to the Recent Apps section or the Dock, or tap on the options button at the top of the app and choose Minimise.

Show and hide recent apps

While running Stage Manager mode, you'll see recent apps running down the side of the screen. Sometimes these recent apps will disappear to make more space for the apps you have running. If this happens, then you can make those recent apps reappear by swiping inwards from the side of the screen.

If you prefer not to see the recent apps panel at all, then you can deactivate it entirely by going to **Settings > Home Screen & Multitasking > Stage Manager**, then toggling **Recent Apps** off.

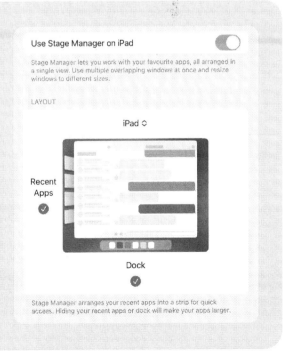

Talk to Siri

Take command of your very own assistant...

Imagine Siri as your very own personal assistant. He (or she depending on your country of origin) can make FaceTime calls for you, dictate emails and messages, make a restaurant reservation, remind you to do things, tell you about movies, make jokes, and much more.

Siri isn't perfect, however. It can't remember interactions from the past, it relies on hearing your voice in a clear manner, and it needs a connection to the internet to work. If you're aware of these limitations and don't mind the odd false request, then Siri can save time and even be a little fun to use.

To enable Siri just hold down the **Power** button on your iPad. If you have an older iPad with a Home button below the screen, press and hold the **Home** button instead. After two seconds you'll hear Siri chime. You can now begin issuing commands, or if you're unsure, stay quiet and after a moment or two you'll see some of the things you can ask Siri.

Speak to Siri

Say out loud, "*What's the weather like today?*" Siri will automatically look for a weather report then tell you what it's going to be like. It's that simple to use Siri.

When you're finished with Siri, tap outside of the Siri bubble to continue using your iPad.

Dictate text with Siri

If you'd like Siri to dictate a message or email, then simply say something like, "*Tell Noah I'll be late*". Siri will automatically create a new message or email to the recipient that says 'I'll be late home tonight'.

Activate Siri via voice command

It's possible to activate Siri by simply saying "*Hey Siri.*" After you hear the recognisable Siri chime, say a command out loud (such as "tell me the time") and Siri will respond – all without your touch. To enable this feature, go to **Settings > Siri & Search**, and turn on **Listen for "Hey Siri"**.

Things you can ask Siri...

"Play something by Monsters and Men"

"Remind me to call Michael at 7."

"Send a message to Dave"

"Set up a meeting with Sarah at 9."

"Email Chris to say I'm running late."

"Show me movies directed by Steven Spielberg"

"How do I get to Tom's?"

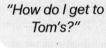

"What is the Microsoft stock price?"

"Do I look fat in this?"

"What are your best chat-up lines?"

"What's 15 plus 26 plus 12 plus 4?"

"Roll the dice."
or
"Flip a coin."

"Schedule a haircut on Tuesday at 1 p.m."

Passwords

Look up or manage your saved passwords...

Whenever you log into a website and enter a username, email address, or password, your iPad will ask if you would like to save these details on the device. If you agree, the next time you go back to the website and try to log in, your iPad will offer to automatically enter those details. It's a great time-saving feature, and it also means you don't have to remember every single password you've ever entered.

Sometimes you might need to take a look at these passwords and login details. Perhaps you're using someone else's computer and can't remember your password, or maybe you've accidentally saved multiple login details for a site and want to tidy them up. Here's how you can access every password and account saved on your iPad in a few steps...

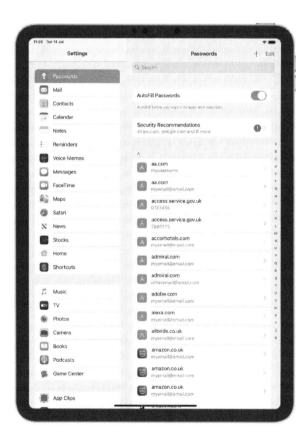

1. Open the **Settings** app, then tap on **Passwords**.

2. Your iPad will automatically scan your face (or ask for your fingerprint), to make sure it's you that's accessing your personal details.

3. You'll then see a list of every website you've ever logged into.

4. You can search for a website, username, email address, or password, by using the search field at the top of the screen.

5. You can add a new set of details by tapping the **plus** (**+**) button in the top-right corner.

6. To delete a set of details, swipe across the account from right to left, then tap the red **Delete** button.

Security Recommendations

Your iPad will automatically look for duplicate passwords, passwords that are easy to guess, or passwords that have leaked onto the web. If it finds any then it will list these at the top of the Passwords panel. Look for **Security Recommendations** below the search bar to find it. If any are available, tap on them, then tap **Change Password on Website** to update your details.

Reset your password using your iPad

If you have forgotten the password for your iPad (also known as your Apple ID), don't worry, as there are a couple of things you can try. The first is to change your password using your iPad. To do this:

1. Open the **Settings** app. It's grey and has a cogwheel in its centre.

2. Tap **[your name]** at the top of the screen, tap **Password & Security**, then tap **Change Password**.

3. If you are signed in to iCloud and have a passcode enabled, then you will be asked to enter the passcode for your device.

4. Follow the onscreen steps to update your password.

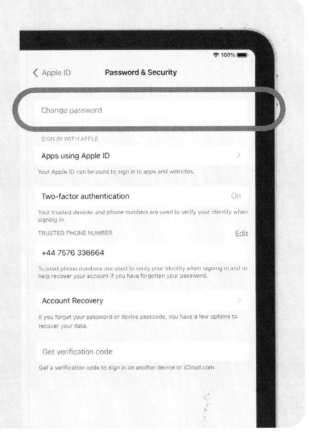

Reset your password on the internet

If the above steps didn't work, then you can try resetting your Apple ID password on the Apple website. To do this:

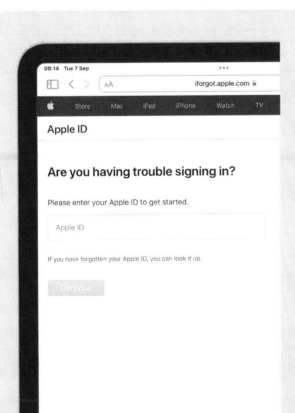

1. Use a web browser (such as Safari) and go to **iforgot.apple.com**

2. Enter your Apple ID. This is usually the email address you use to sign in.

3. Tap **Continue**.

4. If you have two-step verification enabled, then center your phone number, and follow the instructions to reset your password.

5. If you don't have two-step verification enabled, then follow the instructions to reset your password. You may have to enter security questions, or tap a link in an email.

Type like a Pro

Become a master at typing on the iPad keyboard...

Now that you're comfortable typing on the iPad's keyboard, it's time to take a look at some of its more intelligent and advanced features. You might not know from looking at it, but the iPad's keyboard is capable of guessing what you're trying to type. It can even let you enter symbols by flicking your finger upwards from a key. We'll explore all of these features, plus more on the following couple of pages.

Quickly select a word

By double-tapping two fingers on the keyboard you can quickly select a word. Double-tap then drag your finger and you'll be able to select multiple words or sentences.

Use predictive text

Predictive Text attempts to guess the next word you want to type and then offers it as a one-tap option above the keyboard.

To see predictive text in action, open the keyboard then start to type. As you enter each letter, a series of words will appear above the keyboard that guesses what you're trying to say. What makes predictive text really clever is that it learns who you're typing too and changes responses in relation to that person. So if you're talking to a close friend, predicted words will be relaxed and fun, but if it's your boss you'll see more formal and serious words appear.

The only thing I would like to see is that it has a little more variety

| other | one | noise |

q w e r t y u i o p

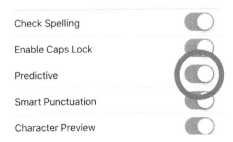

Hide predictive text

If you'd like to hide or enable the predictive text panel just open the **Settings** app and go to **General > Keyboard** then toggle **Predictive** on or off.

Accents and extra keys

To add accents, extra letters and punctuation, **tap and hold** on a key. You'll see extra options and letters appear above your finger. To select one, simply drag your finger to it then let go.

Shortcuts

A shortcut is a quick and efficient way to send a common message. So type "omw" and your iPad will automatically write "On my way!" You'll find more shortcuts, plus the ability to create your own, by opening the **Settings** app, then tapping **Keyboard**.

Slide to type numbers

You can easily add a number by holding your finger on the **123** key, then sliding it to a number that appears.

Format text with the shortcut keys

As you use the iPad's keyboard for typing and entering text you'll probably notice the shortcut keys above they keyboard (if they don't appear then swipe the small grey bar above the keyboard upwards). Usually these enable you to cut, copy, paste, format text and attach images or files with just a tap of a button, but some apps may add further shortcuts.

Easily move the text cursor

If you'd like to quickly move the text cursor to another word or line, **press and hold** on the spacebar then use it as a trackpad with your finger.

Use Key Flick to quickly type symbols

Let's say you're typing a tweet and want to add the hashtag symbol. Using the iPad's Key Flick feature, you can simply press the **S** key then swipe down. You'll then see the key turn to an #, and the symbol appear wherever you're typing.

How to copy, paste, and select text

Discover how to copy something then paste it somewhere else...

Copying and pasting is a great way to move text or content from one app to another. For example, you could copy your address from Contacts and paste it into Safari, or copy a photo and then paste it into an email. The options are endless.

Copy and paste gestures

It takes some practice, but the best way to copy and paste text is to use a series of three-finger gestures. Start by selecting a piece of text (to do this just tap and hold on the text), then perform one of the following gestures:

- **Copy**: Perform a three-finger pinch.
- **Cut**: Three-finger double pinch.
- **Paste**: Three-finger pinch out.
- **Undo**: Swipe left with three fingers.
- **Redo**: Swipe right with three fingers.
- **Access a shortcut menu:** Three-finger tap.

When you successfully use one of the three-finger gestures you'll see a confirmation at the top of your screen.

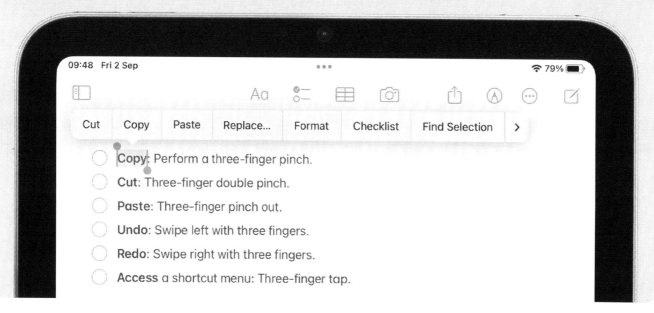

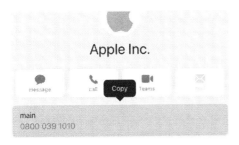

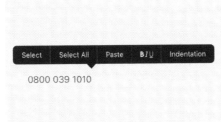

Copy text

Find a source of text on your iPad, perhaps your phone number in Contacts. **Tap and hold** your finger on the number, let go when the magnifying glass appears, then choose **Copy** from the pop-up button.

Paste text

Next, close Contacts and open the Notes app. Create a new note by tapping the **plus** icon, then **tap and hold** on the empty note and choose **Paste**. Your phone number will appear in the new note.

Copy images

To copy an image from the Photos app, open it, tap the **Share** button in the top corner, then choose **Copy Photo**. You can now paste this image into a new email, SMS or iMessage.

Cursor navigation

You can pick up the cursor and drag it somewhere else.

Multiselect text

Quickly select a block of text by dragging your finger across it.

Intelligent text selection

You can select a word with a double tap, a sentence with three taps, and a whole paragraph with four taps.

How to use the Share sheet

Learn how to share something with other people or perform actions...

There's a lot you can do with a photo on your iPad. You can edit it (which we cover in the Photos chapter), share it with friends, hide it, duplicate it, print it, or even save it to the Files app. The same goes for other things on your iPad, like notes, reminders, and web pages. You can share all of these things (and more) by using the Share sheet, which you can access by pressing the Share button. It's usually tucked away in a corner, and it looks like this:

Share something with a friend

When you tap the Share button, you'll see contact suggestions near the top of the panel. These are based on your recent activity with friends and family, so you might see a shortcut to email something, attach it to a message or AirDrop it from one Apple device to another.

App shortcuts

Below the contact suggestions panel are a series of app shortcuts. If you decide to share a photo, you might see shortcuts for sending it within a message, posting it on Facebook, or attaching it within a note.

Other shortcuts

Scroll down the Share sheet, and you'll find a wide range of context-sensitive shortcuts. These are based on the thing you're sharing, so if it's a photo, you'll see shortcuts to hide it, duplicate it, or even make a watch face for your Apple Watch. Decide to share a web page, and you'll see shortcuts for adding a bookmark, finding a piece of on-page text and copying the URL.

Use AirDrop to share files

Send photos or files to friends nearby...

Have you ever wanted to share a photo, note, or video with someone else in the same room? So long as they also have an iPhone, iPad, or Mac, then it's possible to wirelessly transfer something with just a few taps. It works using a combination of Wi-Fi and Bluetooth, and there's no setup required. As a result it's never been quicker or easier to share files with friends, family and colleagues.

Enable AirDrop

To turn on AirDrop go to **Settings** > **General** > **AirDrop**. You can also use Control Centre. To do this open Control Centre, tap and hold on the box in the top-left corner, then tap **AirDrop**. On the following panel you can toggle AirDrop on or off, and choose who to share files with.

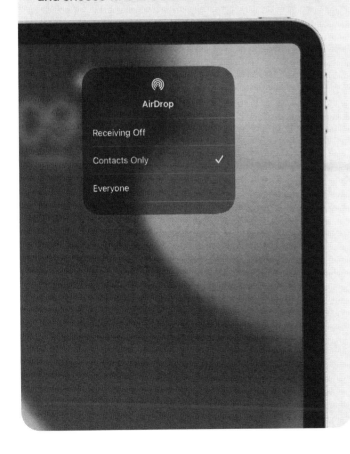

Share a file

Tap the **Share** button while viewing something you'd like to share. It's usually at the bottom of the screen. You'll see the AirDrop button near the middle of the Share sheet. Tap this and you'll see anyone nearby with AirDrop enabled. To share the file with them, just tap on their face or name.

Use your iPad as a second screen for your Mac

Use Sidecar to extend or mirror your desktop onto an iPad...

If you have an iPad released in 2018 or later, then you can use it to extend or mirror your Mac's display. There's no app to install, and everything works wirelessly (although you can plug your iPad into your Mac to keep its battery topped up). Apple calls this feature Sidecar, and it works by extending your Mac's display to one side. Think of it as extra screen space for you to place things. You can also mirror your Mac's display if needed, plus it's possible to use an Apple Pencil to tap and edit things that are placed on the iPad display.

Control your iPad using your Mac

You can easily control your iPad using your Mac's keyboard and Mac. Think of the iPad's display as an extension of your Mac's, meaning you can move the cursor to one side of the screen, and it will appear on the iPad. Here's how to activate this feature:

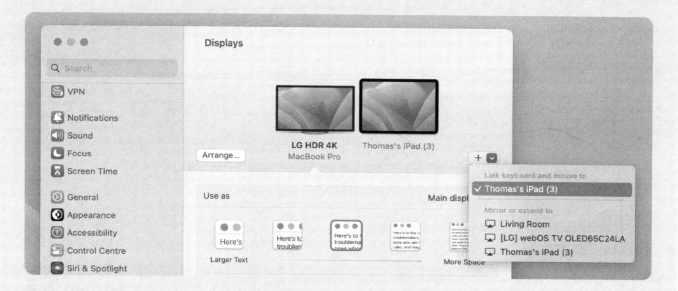

1. Open **System Settings** on your Mac, click **Display**, then click the **plus (+)** button. Using the drop down menu, select your iPad under the **Link keyboard and mouse to** option (see above).

2. You can now move the cursor onto the iPad, and control it using your keyboard and mouse/trackpad.

3. Controlling your iPad with a mouse or trackpad works just like your Mac, so you can scroll through pages and right-click on things. Click on a text entry field, and you can type text using your Mac's keyboard too.

4. To stop controlling your iPad, click on it in the **Displays** panel, then click **Disconnect**.

Extend your Mac's desktop to your iPad

 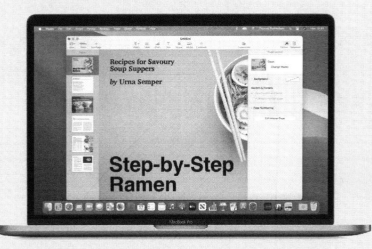

1 Open **System Settings** on your Mac, click **Display**, then click the **plus (+)** button. Using the drop down menu, select your iPad under the **Mirror or extend to** option.

2 You'll see your iPad's display show your Mac's wallpaper, plus a black menu bar running down the side of its display. This is called the Sidebar menu, and it has its own set of controls (see below).

3 You can now drag windows and apps onto the iPad's display and use it as a second monitor for your Mac.

4 To mirror your Mac's screen, rather than extend it, click on your iPad in the **Displays** panel, click on the drop down that says **Extended display**, then choose **Mirror**.

5 To stop extending or mirroring onto your iPad, click on it in the **Displays** panel, then click **Disconnect**.

Sidebar controls

Take a look at the sidebar on your iPad and you'll see a number of controls running down the side of the screen. Here's what each button means:

Tap this to show or hide the menu bar when viewing a window full screen.

This will show or hide the Mac's Dock on the iPad.

Touch and hold to set the **Command** key. Double-tap to lock the key.

Touch and hold to set the **Option** key. Double-tap to lock the key.

Touch and hold to set the **Control** key. Double-tap to lock the key.

Touch and hold to set the **Shift** key. Double-tap to lock the key.

Use Apple Pay to buy things

Leave your wallet in the drawer...

Apple Pay is pretty remarkable. You can use it to pay for apps and music with your iPad, or buy items online without entering your credit card details. On an iPad you can use it online to pay for goods, or within apps when you see the Apple Pay logo, which looks like this:

How to add a card

The first step is to add a credit or debit card, of which you can hold a maximum of eight. Here's how:

1 Open the **Settings** app, go to **Wallet & Apple Pay**, then follow the steps to add a card. If you're trying to add a card which already exists withing your Apple ID account, then you'll only need to enter its security code.

2 Tap **Next** and your bank will authorise and add your card. If your bank needs more details you can add these later via **Settings > Wallet & Apple Pay**.

How to use Apple Pay

If you're using Safari and see the Apple Pay button at the checkout, just tap the button to make the purchase immediately. If you're using an app and see the Apple Pay logo, you might need to toggle a setting that enables Apple Pay first — the app will let you know. Once enabled, tap the **Apple Pay** button, ensure all the details are correct, then use Face ID to confirm your identity.

Choose a default card

The card linked to your Apple ID will automatically be the default card for Apple Pay, but you can change the default card via **Settings > Wallet & Apple Pay > Default Card**.

Remove a credit card

Open the **Settings** app, select **Wallet & Apple Pay**, tap on the card you wish to remove then tap the **Remove Card** button that appears at the bottom of the screen.

Connect to Bluetooth devices

Discover how to pair headphones and other Bluetooth devices...

The speakers in your iPad do a great good job at playing music and audio, but by connecting a set of Bluetooth headphones, you can enjoy audio at a volume level that won't interrupt anyone else. It's not just headphones that you can connect, because the iPad supports a massive number of Bluetooth devices, including gaming controllers, microphones, and even fitness equipment such as treadmills.

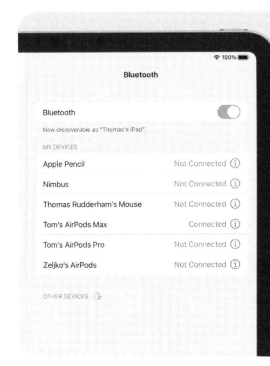

Connect a Bluetooth device

1. Open the **Settings** app, then tap **Bluetooth**.

2. Make sure the **Bluetooth** toggle switch is turned on.

3. Turn on the Bluetooth device you would like to connect to and make it discoverable. If you're not sure how to do that, read the device's instruction manual.

4. The Bluetooth device will appear in the OTHER DEVICES panel. Tap on it to connect. If the device is a computer or a vehicle, then you may need to enter a pairing code.

5. The device will connect and appear in the MY DEVICES panel. It is now ready to use.

Bluetooth options

After a Bluetooth device has been paired, you can often customise it via the Bluetooth Settings panel. For example, if you connect a pair of AirPod Pros, then it's possible to toggle noise cancellation, press and hold options, perform an ear tip fit test, and even which ear acts as a microphone. To find these settings:

1. Open the **Settings** app, then tap **Bluetooth**.

2. Tap the **info (i)** button next to the device.

Swap between devices

If you're listening to music or talking to someone on the phone, and you want to swap from the speaker to your headphones, then:

1. Make sure the Bluetooth device is turned on and connected.

2. Swipe down from the top-right corner of the screen to access Control Centre.

3. Tap the **AirPlay** button. It's in the top-right corner of the music playback box.

4. Tap on the device you'd like to use.

5. While making a phone call, you can also tap the **Audio** button to swap between devices.

Control an Apple TV

Send video and music to your Apple TV...

If you're lucky enough to have an Apple TV, then it's possible to share movies, TV shows, music, and photos on your iPad straight to the television. This means you can start watching a movie on your iPad, then continue it on the TV. You can even mirror the entire iPad screen on the Apple TV, so other people can see what you're doing.

What is an Apple TV?

It's a small black box that plugs into your TV, one that's focused around entertainment, such as TV shows, movies, and music. It even has it's own app store, so you can download services such as Netflix, or even games. Things you can do on an Apple TV include:

- Watch movies, videos, and music
- Look at your photos and slideshows
- Watch third-party video-based apps (such as Netflix)
- Wirelessly stream your iPad's display onto the TV

Use your iPad as a TV remote

To do this, make sure your iPad and Apple TV are connected to the same Wi-Fi, swipe down from the top-right corner of the screen to access Control Centre, then tap the button which looks like a **TV remote**.

1 Press the **Power** button (or **Home** button on a regular iPad) to enable Siri on the TV.

2 Mute the audio by tapping this button.

3 Swipe across the large grey pad to move up, down, left or right.

4 Jump back or forward by 10 seconds.

5 Toggle subtitles.

6 Cycle through TV channels with these two buttons.

Stream video or music to your Apple TV

1. Connect your iPad to the same Wi-Fi connection as the Apple TV.

2. Swipe down from the top-right corner of the screen to access Control Centre.

3. You will see a wireless icon in the top-right corner of the playback control window. Tap it to choose the Apple TV or AirPlay device.

4. If you've never connected your device to the Apple TV before, enter the 4-character passcode that appears on the TV.

To turn off AirPlay, return to Control Centre, tap the playback controls window, tap **AirPlay** then select your device. You can also press the **Back** button on the Apple TV remote.

Mirror your iPad display

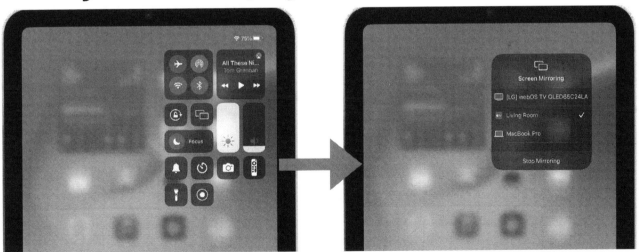

To share your iPad's screen on an Apple TV, swipe down from the top-right corner of the screen to access Control Centre, tap **Screen Mirroring** (it looks like two overlapping rectangles), then choose the Apple TV.

Your iPad will immediately begin mirroring its display. While your screen is being mirrored everything you do on the iPad will appear on-screen, including messages, websites and apps. Note how the images rotates into landscape mode when your turn your device on its side. Also note, that if you view a photo or video while mirroring it will appear full-screen on the TV.

To turn off mirroring, just bring Control Centre back up, tap the white **Apple TV** button, then tap **Stop Mirroring**. Alternatively, lock your iPad via the **power** button and the stream will end, or if you have the Apple TV remote to hand press the **Back** button.

Apple Pencil

Learn about the intuitive Apple Pencil...

There might be times when your fingertip isn't accurate enough for a creative process. Perhaps you'd like to draw a beautiful illustration, but your fingertip is getting in the way; or maybe you'd like to accurately select and manipulate an object that's mere pixels in size. With Apple Pencil, you can do all of that, and more.

That's because the Apple Pencil is sensitive to both tilt and pressure, enabling you to create a range of artistic strokes and effects. You can press harder to create a thicker line, or tilt the Apple Pencil to create subtle curves and shading. Apple Pencil also feels natural to hold, and there's practically no lag between the movement of the Pencil tip and the on-screen response. Using Apple Pencil with the iPad feels intimate, natural and intuitive. There are no buttons to learn, nor gestures to remember, just pick up Apple Pencil and start to draw.

How the Apple Pencil works

Thanks to some incredibly intricate and accurate pressure sensors — as well as two tilt sensors – the Pencil can calculate the exact orientation and angle of your hand. Your iPad recognises when an Apple Pencil is being used, so to prevent spurious inputs it turns off Multi-Touch recognition to stop your palm and fingers from sending signals to the display. All this technology means you can quickly draw and sketch lines without the iPad missing a curve or swivel.

Tap sensitive

Whenever you want to change tools within an app, just double-tap the Apple Pencil. Using the Notes app, you can swap from the pen to the eraser with just two taps, and with third-party apps, you can configure the double-tap feature to suit your needs.

If you want to quickly get into the Notes app on your iPad, then tap the screen with the tip of the Apple Pencil and you'll automatically unlock the device and jump straight into the Notes app.

It's magnetic

The first generation of Apple Pencil was a bit fiddly to charge. First, you had to pull off its cap, then plug the top of the Pencil into the Lightning Port on the bottom of the iPad. The second generation of Apple Pencil supports wireless charging; so to charge it, just snap the Pencil to the side of your iPad.

The magnet is stronger than you might think too, so you can carry your iPad, or even shake it, and the Pencil won't drop off.

First generation Apple Pencil

The Apple Pencil detailed above supports either the iPad Pro, iPad Air, or iPad mini.

If you have an original iPad that was manufactured in 2020 or later, then you can use the original Apple Pencil to sketch and tap. It's not magnetic, so you'll need to pull the cap off then plug the Pencil into the charge port on your iPad, but the original Apple Pencil is just as fun and creative as the second generation.

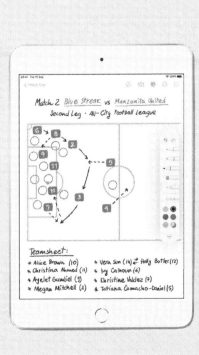

How to use the Apple Pencil

Write, annotate, and draw with the Apple Pencil...

Using the Apple Pencil to tap, annotate and draw, feels surprisingly natural. Think of writing on a notepad or a clipboard, and you'll get the idea. Nevertheless, there are some clever features built into the Apple Pencil that you might now know about, such as a dedicated toolbar, a double-tap, and the ability to draw perfect shapes...

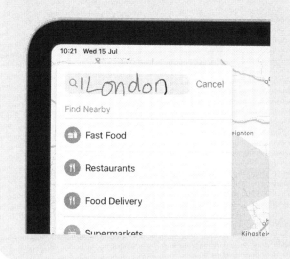

How to enter text

Whenever you see a text box, such as the web address field in Safari, or the search box in Maps, tap on the field using your Apple Pencil, then use handwriting to enter text.

If you need extra space to write then don't worry about going outside of the field - you can write anywhere on the screen, and your iPad will know that you're entering text using handwriting. As you finish each word, your iPad will automatically recognise it and enter it as text in the field that you selected.

The toolbar

A helpful toolbar will appear at the bottom of the screen whenever your use an Apple Pencil. If it gets in the way of something, then you can drag it to the side of the screen. You can also shrink it down to a small ellipse by tapping the options button on the right-side of the toolbar, then toggling **Auto-minimise** on. Here's a quick overview of each button you'll find in the toolbar:

1. Tap this button to undo what you just wrote.

2. Tap this to redo a change.

3. This opens the on-screen keyboard, letting you quickly type other than use handwriting.

4. Tap on this ellipse button to access further options for the toolbar.

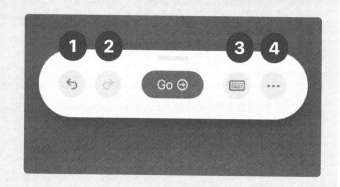

Enter a space

If you'd like to add a space in-between words, **tap and hold** between words as you write. This can be helpful if your handwriting is small and the iPad is accidentally merging words.

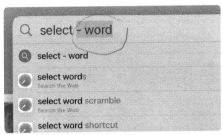

Select text

To quickly select words or entire sentences, just **draw a circle** around them using the Apple Pencil.

Delete words

You can get rid of something you've written with the Apple Pencil by **scratching it out**.

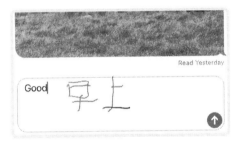

Swap languages

Your iPad will automatically recognise whether you're writing in English or Chinese. This means you can change languages mid-sentence, and your iPad will automatically enter the correct text or symbols.

Select hand-written text

While writing with the Pencil in the Notes app, **tap and hold** on a word, and in the pop-up field which appears, select **Copy as Text**. You can then paste the text somewhere else on your iPad.

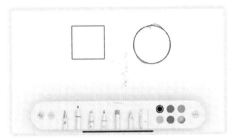

Draw perfect shapes

While using your Apple Pencil in the Notes app, draw the outline of a shape then hold for a second. Your iPad will automatically recognise what you've scribbled, then turn it into a perfect shape.

Customise double-tap

You can double-tap on the Apple Pencil to perform a number of actions:
- Switch between the current tool and the eraser.
- Switch between the current tool and the last used tool.
- Open the colour palette.

To choose one of these, open the **Settings** app, select **Apple Pencil**, then make a choice using the DOUBLE-TAP panel.

Smart Keyboard Folio

Type comfortably with a physical keyboard...

There's no denying that writing on the iPad is a great experience. The display is large enough to accommodate a full-sized keyboard, while Multi-Touch capabilities let you access accent keys, emoji's and even turn the keyboard into a giant trackpad. So why would you want to buy the Smart Keyboard?

Well, for one it enables you to see a full-screen view of your document, art, or work. That's because as soon as you attach the Smart Keyboard, your iPad automatically recognises it and turns off the on-screen keyboard. Second, the Smart Keyboard acts as a robust cover for your iPad, protecting the screen when not in use while also acting as a stand for propping up the device during a movie.

So how does it work? A highly-durable fabric is laser-ablated to form the shape of each key. This provides a spring-like tension which mimics the feel of a traditional key, while eliminating the need for traditional mechanisms. The fabric of the keyboard is water and stain-resistant, but only 4 millimeters thin to ensure the keyboard is slim and lightweight. Beneath the top layer is a conductive layer of fabric which reads each keystroke then seamlessly communicates each press back to the iPad. It does this instantly, and without the need for wires, so you can enjoy a simple yet technologically advanced way to type.

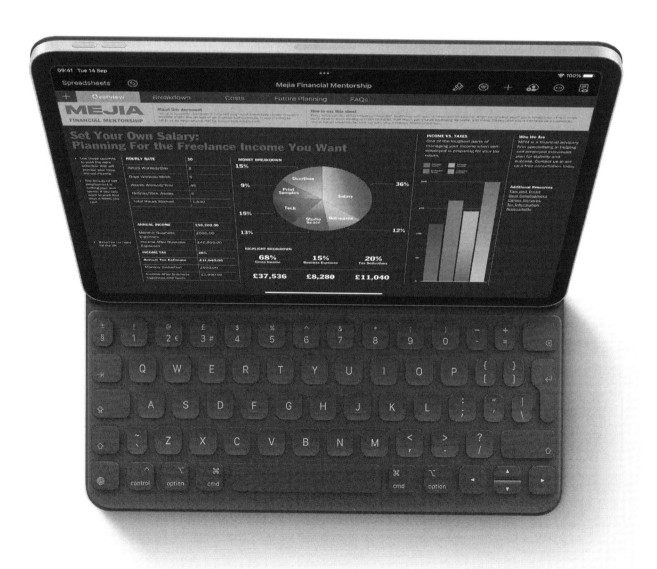

Shortcuts bar

When the Smart Keyboard is attached to your iPad, text-based apps such as Notes, Mail, and Pages automatically recognise the keyboard and offer a full-screen view of your work. However, look at the bottom of the screen and you'll see the shortcuts bar. You can use this to perform commands with the iPad, swap between apps, or access the search bar.

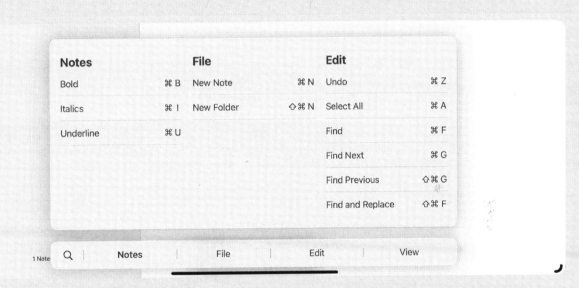

Keyboard shortcuts

While using a text-based app, hold down the **Command (cmd ⌘)** key, and you'll see which shortcuts work with the on-screen app. As an example, here are just a few of the shortcuts that work with Notes:

⌘ N	New Note
⌘ P	Print the current note
⌘ Z	Undo the last change
⌘ V	Paste text or imagery
⌥ ⇧ ⌘ V	Paste text and match the current style
⌘ A	Select All
⌥ ⌘ F shift W	Search through all your notes
⌘ F	Search the current note
⌘ Z	End editing the note

Magic Keyboard for iPad Pro

A full-sized keyboard with a laptop-like trackpad...

The Magic Keyboard is an amazing companion for your iPad Pro or 2020 iPad Air. It features the best typing experience ever on iPad, with a scissor mechanism keyboard, a trackpad that opens up new ways to work with iPadOS, a USB-C port for pass-through charging, and front and back protection. The Magic Keyboard also features a floating cantilever design, allowing you to attach iPad Pro magnetically and smoothly adjust it to the perfect viewing angle for you.

Comfortable typing

Full-size, backlit keys ensure it's easy to type on the Magic Keyboard, even in the dark. The Magic Keyboard also features the same scissor mechanism found on the MacBook keyboard with 1 mm of travel, so typing is responsive yet quiet.

Floating cantilever design

The iPad appears to float over the Magic Keyboard, suspended in the air by the a cantilever mecahnism. The angle of the iPad can also be adjusted for the perfect viewing angle.

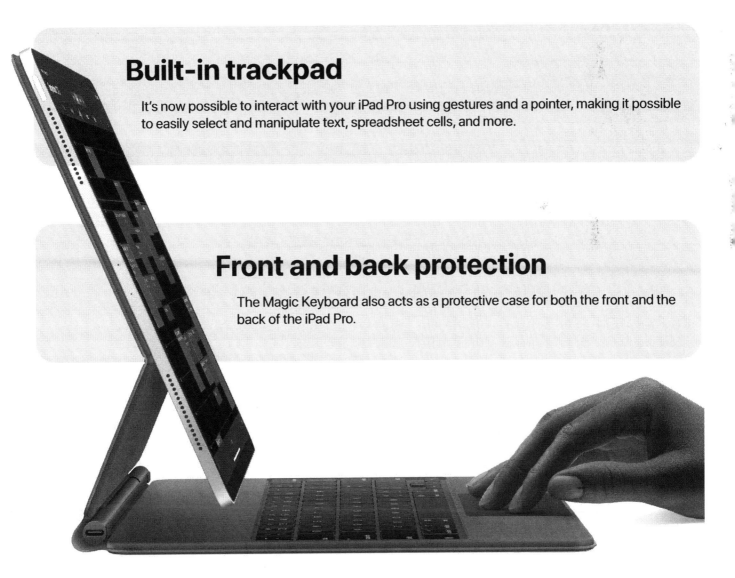

Built-in trackpad

It's now possible to interact with your iPad Pro using gestures and a pointer, making it possible to easily select and manipulate text, spreadsheet cells, and more.

Front and back protection

The Magic Keyboard also acts as a protective case for both the front and the back of the iPad Pro.

How to use a trackpad or mouse

Use a pointer to select objects, manipulate text, and more...

The iPad has always been a versatile device for day-to-day tasks such as browsing the web and creating basic documents, but with a trackpad or mouse, it's pretty much a replacement for the traditional computer. That's because a trackpad or mouse makes it possible to easily select text, move objects, and even manipulate spreadsheet cells. Best of all, iPadOS supports a number of gestures which enable you to fully control every part of the iPad experience, using just the trackpad or mouse. To get started, it's recommended that you use one of these three accessories:

Magic Keyboard (for iPad Pro)

This full-sized keyboard includes scissor mechanism keys and a large Multi-Touch trackpad. It also includes a USB-C port for passthrough charging and front and back protection.

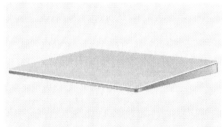

Magic Trackpad 2

Traditionally included with the iMac, this stand-alone trackpad can automatically connect to the iPad using Bluetooth.

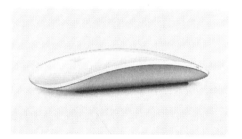

Magic Mouse 2

Another accessory traditionally available for the Mac. If you've used a desktop computer in the past, then this will be a very familiar accessory to use with your iPad.

How to connect a Magic Trackpad or Mouse

To connect the Magic Trackpad or Mouse to the iPad, open the **Settings** app, tap **Bluetooth**, then select the accessory. If you don't see it, make sure to unpair it from your Mac first.

The basics of using the pointer

With a trackpad or mouse connected to your iPad, you'll see a circular dot on the screen. This is called the pointer, and it moves around the screen as you slide your finger across the trackpad or move the mouse.

- **The pointer only appears when you need it.** The pointer isn't persistent at all times, instead only appearing when you're touching the trackpad or moving the mouse.

- **It can change shape based on what it's pointing at.** The pointer changes shape to be the size of the button or app below it, and if you move it over text, it turns into a thin vertical line. You can disable this by going to **Settings > Accessibility > Pointer Control**, then toggling **Pointer Animations** off.

Wake your iPad

You can wake up your iPad by using a trackpad or mouse. Just click it and you'll see your iPad wake up.

Unlock your iPad

Move the pointer to the Home bar at the bottom of the screen and you'll automatically unlock your iPad.

Right-click

You can right-click on apps, text, and objects to access the same secondary menu found when tapping and holding.

Return to the Home Screen

To go home using the trackpad, swipe up with three fingers. If using a mouse, move the pointer to the Home bar then click on it.

Access the Dock

To quickly access the Dock at anytime, move the pointer to the bottom of the screen.

Access Control Centre

To adjust settings or control music at any time, click the **status icons** in the upper-right corner to bring up Control Centre.

The multitasking screen

You can jump between apps or force-close them by swiping up and holding with three fingers.

Jump between apps

You can swipe between open apps by swiping left and right with three fingers.

Slide Over apps

Move the pointer over the Slide Over app, then swipe using three fingers to jump between apps.

The basics of using apps

Learn what an app is, how to open and close apps, plus more...

Each app on your iPad specialises in a particular task, so if you want to take a photo, just tap on the Camera app; and if you want to send a text message, then tap on the Messages app. You can never break your iPad by opening the wrong app, so feel free to open each app to see what it does and how it works.

Open an app

You can open any app on your iPad by lightly tapping on its icon. Just a quick tap of your fingertip is all that's needed.

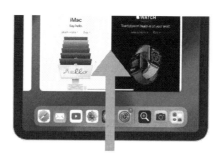

Close an app

When you're ready to close an app and return to the home screen, just press the **Home** button on a regular iPad, or swipe upwards from the bottom of the screen on an iPad Pro or iPad Air.

Force an app to quit

If you're using an app and it stops working, swipe upwards from the bottom of the screen then stop after a few inches. You'll see a grid of recently opened apps appear. To force quit the app you were just using, slide it upwards off the top of the screen.

Delete an app

If you've downloaded an app but want to remove it, simply tap and hold on the app icon, wait a moment, then tap the **minus (-)** button that appears when the app starts to wiggle.

Tap and hold for options

You can **tap and hold** on most things on your iPad to access additional options, so tap and hold on an app and you can rearrange it or quickly jump to something within the app.

Create a folder of apps

Simply **tap and hold** on an app, wait until it starts to jiggle, then drag it on top of another app. This will create a folder of apps. You can rename a folder by tapping and holding on its name.

How to remove default apps

How to get rid of the apps you never use...

Even the staunchest Apple fan will admit that some of the default apps on iPad are unnecessary. After all, not everyone is a stock analyst, and we don't all use the Shortcuts app to create custom commands. It's possible to organise any unnecessary apps into a specific folder then forget about them, or alternatively, you can delete these apps and forget about them entirely. To do this simply **tap and hold** the app icon that you'd like to remove, then when it starts to wiggle tap the **X** button. You'll see a warning that any local data and app settings will be removed too. If you're happy to proceed tap **Remove** and the app will vanish from your screen.

Default apps you can remove...

- Reminders
- Stocks
- Calendar
- Contacts
- Facetime
- Find My
- Home
- Books
- iCloud Drive
- iTunes Store
- Mail
- Maps
- Music
- News
- Notes
- Podcasts

There are some downsides to removing default apps. For example, if you delete the Mail app then tap an email address within Safari, you'll see a pop-up window which suggests you restore the Mail app.

Restore a deleted default app

Wondering how you can restore a deleted app such as Notes, Stocks or Find Friends? It's easy, just open the **App Store**, search for the app you'd like to restore then tap the **iCloud** button. In an instant (remember these apps aren't actually deleted from your iPad) the app will be back on the Home Screen and ready to use.

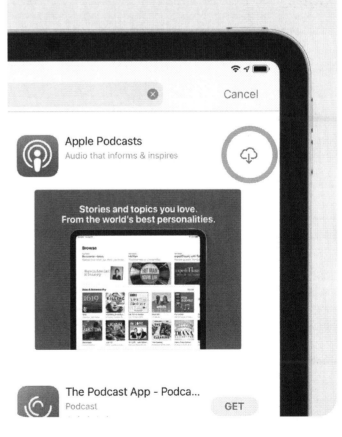

Manage your apps

Manage, hide, and find apps on your iPad...

As you begin to use your iPad, you'll quickly notice that you don't need to use all of its apps. Maybe you don't care about Stocks, or maybe you never need to listen to Podcasts. Whatever the reason, you'll soon want to start managing, hiding, or even deleting apps.

Hide apps

If there's an app on your iPad that you don't need, **tap and hold** on its icon until a small pop-up window appears, then tap **Remove App**. You'll be offered two choices:

1. **Remove from Home Screen**. Tap this option and the app won't be deleted. Instead, it will be moved to the App Library (see across the page for more).

2. **Delete**. Tap this and the app will be permanently deleted from your iPad. If you change your mind at a later date then you can always re-install it via the App Store.

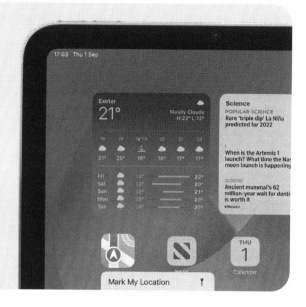

Hide entire pages of apps

If you've accumulated a large number of apps then you might end up with multiple pages of them spread across your Home Screen. Scrolling from one page to another can soon become a chore.

If this has happened to you then don't worry, as it's possible to quickly hide entire pages of apps. You can even bring them back at a later date if you wish. Here's how it works:

1. Go to the Home Screen, then **tap and hold** on an empty space below your apps.

2. When the apps start to jiggle, tap the **series of dots** at the bottom of the screen. It looks like this:

2. You'll enter the Edit Pages view. To hide a page, tap on the **tick** button below it. You can re-enable the same page at a later time by returning to this view and re-ticking it.

Visit the App Library

Think of the App Library as an organised collection of every app installed on your iPad. Those collections are made automatically, with the top two spots reserved for Suggestions and Recently Added, followed by categories of apps based on your recent activitity. To find the App Library, swipe towards the left from the Home Screen, then keep going until the App Library appears. You can also tap the App Library button on the far right side of the Dock.

The App Library

When the App Library fades into view it shows a structured view of every app on your iPad. You can tap on an app to open it immediately, or tap on a smaller group of apps to expand that view.

See a list view

Pull the App Library view downwards with your finger and the list view will appear. You can scroll freely through it, scrub quickly by sliding your finger along the right-hand letters, or jump to a specific letter by tapping on the coresponding letter.

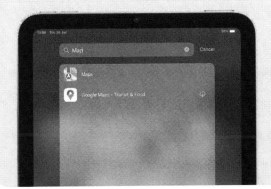

Search for an app

To search for a specific app, simply tap on the search field at the top of the App Library then start typing a few letters. Results will appear instantly as you write.

Explore the App Store

Discover an unlimited number of amazing apps for your iPad...

Your iPad is a pretty amazing tablet straight from the box, with a great web browser, note-taking app and photo editor; but if you'd like to do something specific, such as watch Netflix, make a Zoom video call, or play a video game, then you'll need to visit the App Store where there are millions more apps to discover.

Think of the App Store as a shopping mall, but for apps. To find it, look for this icon:

Open the App Store, and it's hard not to be overwhelmed by the sheer number of apps, tools, and games available. You'll initially see highlighted apps for the day. This is curated by a team within Apple, and they usually handpick some of the most inventive and fun apps out there. Look at the bottom of the screen, and you'll see shortcuts to the latest games, apps, Apple Arcade (a subscription service focused around games), and a search shortcut which lets you look for a specific app.

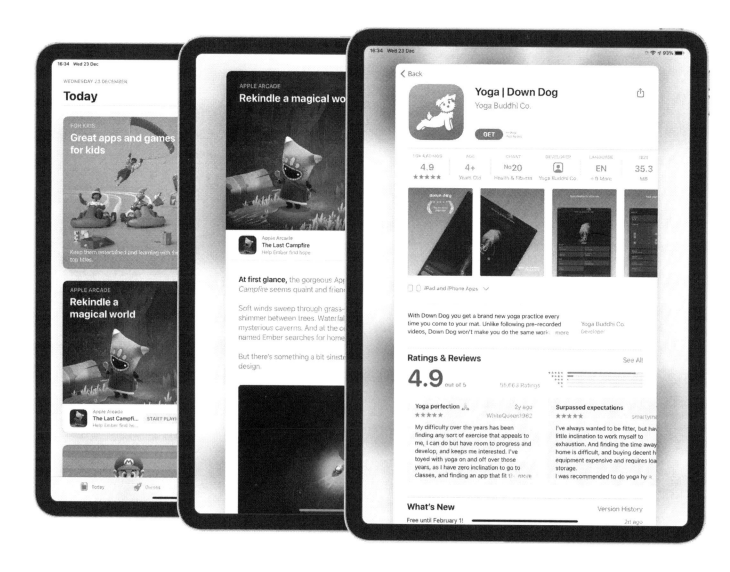

How to install an app

To install an app, just tap the **GET** button if it's a free app, or the **price** button if it's a paid app.

After you've entered your Apple ID password, the app will be added to the Home screen of your iPad.

In-app purchases

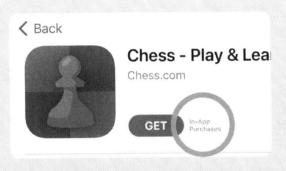

Wondering why that amazing-looking app is free? Chances are it has in-app purchases. These are optional purchases you can make within an app to unlock extra features. To see if an app includes in-app purchases, look for the text "In-App Purchases" next to the get/price button.

Data privacy

Many apps within the App Store will want to track you in various ways. Some will want to look through your contact information, while others might want to access your photos, or even your shopping history. You can see how an app tracks you by looking for it in the App Store, then scrolling down to the **App Privacy** section. From here you will see a breakdown of what the app does with your privacy. If you don't like what you see, then you can ignore the app and look for another.

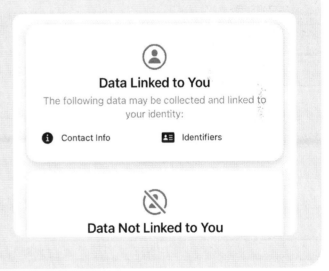

How to review an app

Want to tell others about how great (or terrible) an app is? First make sure you've already downloaded the app, then head over to its page on the App Store, scroll down to the **Reviews** section, then tap **Write a Review**.

Use Safari to browse the web

Visit websites, organise tabs, customise your experience, and more...

Browsing the web using Safari on iPad is a wonderful experience. Websites look stunning on the large display, with crisp text and vivid images, and they load in an instant. Thanks to the all-new multitasking capabilities, it's also possible to browse the web while reading your emails, checking out the latest tweets or making a FaceTime call.

This chapter will explain how the Safari app works, how to take advantage of its features and how you can customise the experience to best suit your needs.

You'll find the Safari app already installed on your iPad. To locate it, just unlock your iPad then tap on this icon:

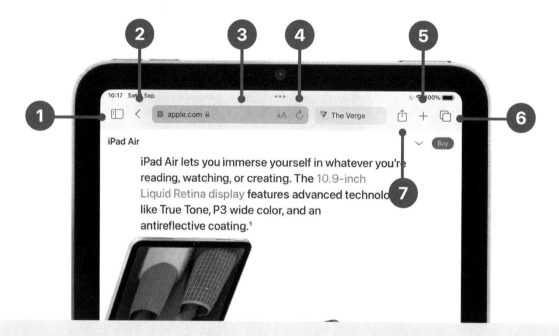

The basics

1 Tap the **sidebar** button to access your tab groups (see across page), open a Private tab, see shared content, access your bookmarks, reading list, and browsing history.

2 Use these arrows to go back a page, or forward a page.

3 Tap the **address** field to search the web or type a website address.

4 Tap this curved arrow to refresh the page. **Tap and hold** to view the desktop version of a site.

5 You can open a new tab window by tapping this button.

6 Tap the **Tabs** button to view all of the tabs open on your iPad.

7 Tap the **Share** button to send a webpage to another iPad, message a link, email a link, print the page and much more.

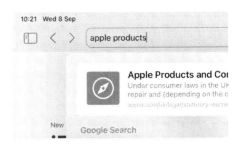

Enter a website address

To visit a website, tap on the **address field** and enter an URL using the on-screen keyboard. Tap the blue **Go** button on the keyboard to visit the site.

How to search the internet

The address bar in Safari also acts as a search engine, so to search the web for any question or search term, just type your query into the address bar at the top of the screen.

Search suggestions

As you type into the address bar, notice that Safari offers search suggestions in realtime. Tap on a suggestion or the blue **Go** button on the keyboard to confirm your query.

Use tabs to visit more than one website

Think of a tab as a single view of a webpage. You can have as many tabs open on your iPad as you like, but you can only view one at a time. To open a new tab view, press the **plus (+)** button at the top of the screen.

Explore and close tabs

To see an overview of all your tabs, tap the **tabs** button in the very top-right corner of the screen. To close a tab, press the small **X** button in it's top-right corner.

Create a group of tabs

If you have many tabs open on your iPad, then it might be a good idea to group them into categories. By doing this, you could create a tab group for home, a tab group for work, and a tab group for everything else.

To create a group of tabs, tap the **sidebar** button, then tap the **new tab group** button in the upper right corner. To create a new tab group from scratch, tap **New Empty Tab Group**. Alternatively, you can create a tab group using all the tabs currently open by tapping **New Tab Group from (number) Tabs**.

Turn over for more on tabs...

Jump between tab groups

To jump to another group of tabs, tap the **name** of the current tab group in the top left corner, then make a choice. You can also press the **sidebar** button and then select a group.

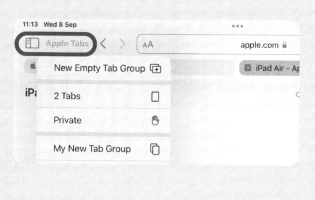

Add a page to a tab group

If you're in one group of tabs, and wish to save a page to another group of tabs, **tap and hold** on the **tabs** button in the top right corner, select **Move to Tab Group**, then make a choice.

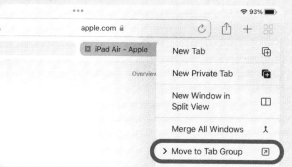

Delete a tab group

To delete a group of tabs, tap the **sidebar** button, then swipe from right to left across the group you wish to delete. Next, tap the **red trash** button and confirm.

Adjust website settings

To remove ads and clutter from a webpage, tap the **AA** button, then tap **Show Reader View**. You can also adjust text size and website settings by tapping **AA**.

See content shared with you

If someone has shared a link with you via the Messages or AirDrop, then you can always find it at a later date by opening the **sidebar** and then choosing **Shared with You**.

Enable Private Browsing

To browse the web without saving any history, searches, or passwords, tap the **sidebar** button, then choose **Private**.

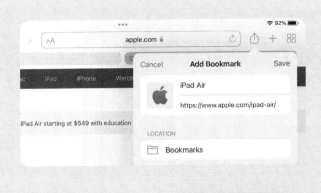

Add a bookmark

If you visit a website regularly then it's a good idea to bookmark it. This lets you easily re-visit the website by either opening a new tab, or by tapping the **sidebar** button and then **Bookmarks**. To add a new bookmark, tap the **Share** button at the top of the screen, then choose **Add Bookmark**.

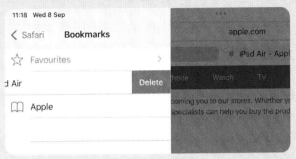

Manage your bookmarks

To quickly visit your bookmarks, tap the **sidebar** button, then choose **Bookmarks**.

To remove or edit a Bookmark, swipe across it from right to left, then tap **Delete**.

Add a favourite

Whenever you tap on the address bar or open a new tab, Safari will display your favourite websites. This is a helpful way to access your favouite sites without having to type its URL each time.

To add a new favourite, tap the **share** button and then choose **Add to Favourites**.

To remove a saved favourite, **tap and hold** on it and then choose **Delete**.

Quickly type domain URLs

There's no need to manually type .com, .co.uk or .net. Instead, touch and hold the **.com** button on the keyboard to choose from a variety of domain suffixes.

Translate a page

To translate a web page from French, Spanish, Simplified Chinese, German, Russian, or Brazilian Portuguese, to your own language, tap the **AA** button at the top of the screen, then choose **Translate to English**.

Change the search engine

By default, Safari searches the web using results from Google. If you'd rather search using Yahoo!, Bing, or DuckDuckGo, go to **Settings > Safari > Search Engine**.

Access tabs open on your iPhone or Mac

Using iCloud, tabs are automatically synced across all of your Apple devices, such as your iPhone, Mac, and iPad. To access them on your iPad, tap the **address bar**, then scroll down the pop-up panel which appears below it. Eventually, you'll see any tabs open on your other devices at the bottom of the panel.

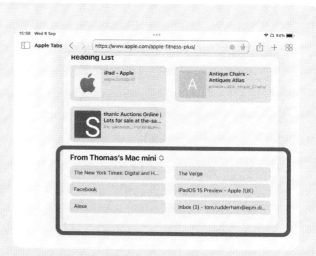

See your browsing history

If you want to re-visit a page from earlier, then open the **sidebar** and tap **History**. A search bar at the top will let you look for a specific page, or you can simply scroll down through your history.

Delete a page from your history

Swipe across a page in the sidebar from right to left, and you'll be able to remove it from your browsing history.

Clear your browsing history

If you need to clear all of your browsing history, go to **Settings > Safari**, then tap the **Clear History and Website Data** button.

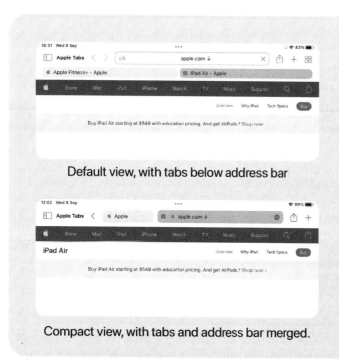

Default view, with tabs below address bar

Compact view, with tabs and address bar merged.

Simplify the tab bar

By default, tabs open on your iPad appear below the address bar at the top of the screen. This makes it easy to distinguish the address bar from the tabs, but it takes up a lot of space at the top of the screen.

You can simplify this by merging the address bar with tabs, resulting in a cleaner look which gives the page below more room to show content. To this go to **Settings > Safari**, then toggle **Compact Tab Bar** on.

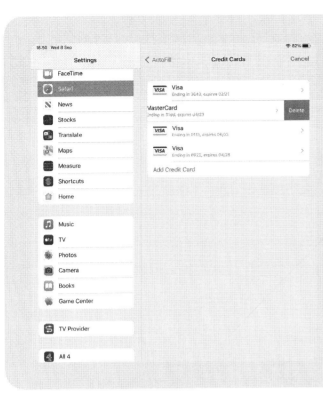

Edit saved credit card details

The first time you enter credit card details into Safari, it will ask you if you would like to save the card details on your iPad. Agree to this, and the credit card number, expiry date, and account name will be saved. The 3-digit code on the back will not be saved for security purposes. By saving these details, the next time you try to buy something Safari will auto-fill your card's details, saving you considerable time.

If you would like to edit any saved credit card details, go to **Settings** > **Safari** > **Autofill**, then tap **Credit Cards**. To edit the details of a card, tap on, it then choose **Edit**. To delete a card, swipe across it from right to left and then choose **Delete**.

Search a web page for text

To find a piece of text on a webpage, tap the **Share** button, then choose **Find on Page**. Next, use the keyboard to search for a word or phrase and it will be highlighted on the page.

Block ads and junk from slowing down the web

Using Safari it's possible to install "extensions" which prevent adverts from loading on web pages. To install and activate a content blocker, open the App Store and search for "*content blocker*". Once you've chosen an app, install it, then go to **Settings** > **Safari** > **Extensions** and toggle the blocker on.

Save a page for later

If you don't have time to finish reading a page or article, tap the **share** button and choose **Add to Reading List**. The page will then be saved to your Reading List, so you can read it at a later time or date. To access your Reading List, open the **sidebar** then choose **Reading List**.

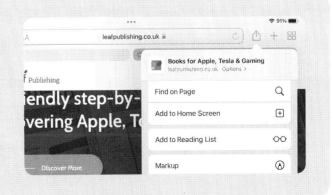

Check your email

Compose messages, organise your inbox, and more...

Alongside the Messages app, Mail must come close to being on the most used apps on iPad. That's because if you're serious about doing things on the web, like shopping or registering for services, then there's no way to avoid having an email address — it's a basic requirement for so many things.

Thankfully, the Mail app on iPad is easy to use and gets straight to the point. It's designed with a clean, white interface that helps you focus on what's important: your emails. Buttons are coloured blue, and basic Multi-Touch gestures enable you to delete messages, flag them and more.

You'll find the Mail app already installed on your iPad. To find it, just unlock your iPad then tap on this icon:

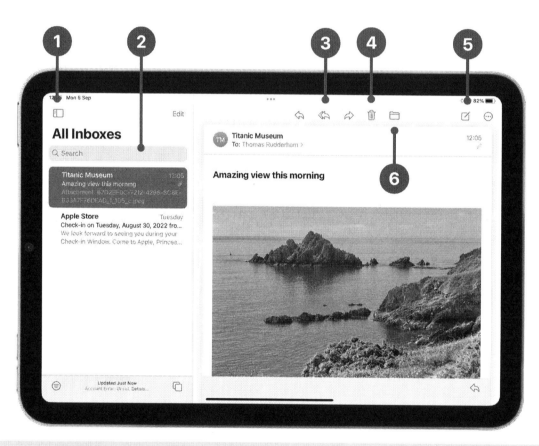

The basics

1 Use this back arrow to return to the Mailboxes screen, where you can access your Drafts, Sent, Junk, and Trash mailboxes.

2 Looking for a particular email or recipient? Pull the inbox down then use the **search box** to quickly find it.

3 Reply, reply to all, or forward an email.

4 Delete an email by tapping the **Trash** icon.

5 Tap this button to create a new email.

6 Tap this icon to move an email into a folder.

Quickly format text

If you'd like to bold, italicise or underline a word or sentence, highlight the text then tap on the **option** arrow. Next, tap **BIU** and select the format you wish to use.

Attach images and videos

To attach an image within an email, tap and hold where you want it to go, then tap the **photo** button above the keyboard. There's also a **camera** button for taking a photo on the spot.

Attach a file from iCloud

To attach a document, PDF, zip file, or an image saved in iCloud, tap on the **document** button above the keyboard.

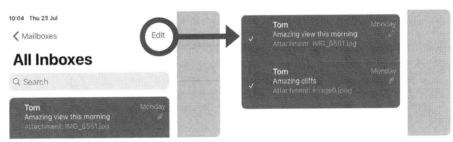

Format text

While composing an email, tap the Aa button above the keyboard to access a wide range of text editing tools, such as font family, colour, and layout.

Delete multiple emails

While viewing your inbox, tap the blue **Edit** text in the top right corner. Next, tap on the messages you'd like to delete. Once you're happy with the selection, tap the **Bin** button in the bottom-corner.

Move or mark multiple emails

Follow the steps above, but instead of deleting the selected messages select either **Mark** or **Move** at the bottom of the screen. Mark enables you to flag the messages, mark them as unread or move them to the Junk folder. Move enables you to store the emails in a separate folder from the Inbox.

See contact details

While reading an email, tap on the name of the contact at the top of the message and you'll see their details in full.

Schedule an email

If you would like to send an email at a particular time, tap and hold on the blue **send** button, then choose to either send it straight away or send it at a suggested time.

If you would like to choose a specific time, tap and hold on the **send** button, choose **Send Later...** then pick a specific date and time.

Un-send an email

If you accidentally send an email it's possible to unsend it - but you only have 10 seconds to do so. Here's how it works:

1 Immediately after sending an email, look at the bottom of your screen.

2 Tap **Undo Send,** and the email you just sent will reappear as a draft.

3 You can now cancel the email, or make changes before sending it again.

4 If you'd like to give yourself more time to undo an email, go to **Settings** > **Mail** > **Undo Send Delay**, and choose up to 30 seconds.

Get email reply notifications

Waiting for an important reply to an email? You can receive a notification when it arrives by opening the email message, tapping the **arrow** button in the bottom corner, then **Notify Me...**

Save a contact to your device

If you've received an email from someone and would like to save their contact details to your iPhone, then tap on their **name** at the top of the email, then select either **Create New Contact** or **Add to Existing Contact.**

Mark an email as Unread

Sometimes it's helpful to mark emails as unread so they can be later re-read or referenced. To do this, swipe the message towards the right, then choose **Unread**.

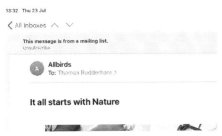

Automatically unsubscribe

If you receive an unsolicited marketing email and want to quickly unsubscribe, open the message then tap the **Unsubscribe** text at the top of the screen.

Forward an email

To quickly forward an email to someone else, tap the **arrow** button in the bottom-right corner, then tap **Forward**.

Print an email

To print an email, tap the **forward arrow** button at the bottom of the screen, then tap **Print**. Select a wireless printer then tap **Print**.

Attach a drawing

You can attach a drawing to an email by tapping the **pencil** button above the keyboard. While drawing, you can choose from a variety of tools, such as a pencil, felt tip, marker, or ruler. You can further customise a tool by tapping on it, so tap on the felt tip tool and you'll be able to adjust the line thickness and opacity.

Delete an email with a swipe

Erasing emails can become a chore, so to speed up the process, simply **swipe your finger right-to-left** across the email message while in the Inbox.

More email options

After swiping an email from right-to-left, tap the **More** button and you'll see a selection of controls appear. Options include Reply, Forward, Mark, Notify, and Move.

Save a draft email

If you're composing an email and you're not ready to send it yet, drag the email down to the bottom of the screen. It'll stay there, below the rest of your emails, until you tap on it to continue the draft.

Chat using Messages

Send messages, photos, emojis, and even animated faces...

You might not think of the iPad as a device for sending messages, but that's exactly what you can do with the Messages app. For those times when your iPhone isn't to hand, it can prove to be a surprisingly fun and useful app, and because your messages are synced across all of your Apple devices, you can start a conversion on your iPad and continue it later on your iPhone.

To find the Messages app on your iPad, just look for the green app icon with a speech bubble:

The basics

1 Tap the **New Message** button to start a conversation.

2 Tap on a persons name or image to see more details about them.

3 Tap the **Camera** button to take a photo on the spot, or tap the **Photos** button to send an image from your library.

4 Tap and hold the **Microphone** button to dictate a message. Let go when you've finished recording.

5 Access a variety of characterful emojis by tapping this button.

6 If you need to move the cursor around, tap and hold on the **spacebar** to turn the keyboard into a trackpad.

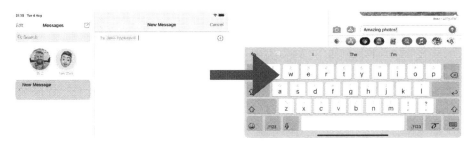

Send a new message

Tap the **New Message** icon in the top-right corner of the Messages app. In the **To**: field, begin to type the name of a contact, their email address or a phone number. If the contact already exists on your iPad then you'll see their name appear above the keyboard. You can tap on this entry to automatically fill the To: field, or continue to enter the recipient's details until complete.

Once you've entered a recipients contact details, tap the **text entry** field just above the keyboard, then type a message. Once you're ready to send, tap the **blue arrow** button (sometimes it's green if the other person doesn't have an iPad or iPhone), and the message will be sent.

Send a photo

If you'd like to send a photo to someone, tap the **Photos** button above the keyboard. A panel will then appear showing your recent photos. If you need to find an older image, drag the panel upwards with your finger. To send multiple photos, tap on each one then tap **Add** near the top of the screen. The photos will then be sent as a stack of images.

Delete a chat

There are two ways to remove chat conversations from the Messages app. The simplest is to **swipe right-to-left** across the chat conversation in the sidebar. Alternatively, tap the **Edit** button at the top of the Messages screen, select the conversation/s that you wish to delete, then tap the **Delete** button.

Pin contacts

If you talk to someone regularly, then it's a good idea to pin them to the top of the Messages home page. To do this, swipe across their chat conversation from left-to-right, then tap the yellow **pin** button. To remove them at a later date, simply tap and hold on their icon, then choose **Unpin**.

Create your very own Memoji

With the Memoji feature, you can create your very own 3D avatar, then use it to send fun animated messages to friends and family. Here's how it works:

1 Open the **Messages** app, then tap on the **Animoji** button. It looks like a cartoon face with a yellow box around it.

2 Tap the **+** button to create a custom Memoji. Scroll to the left if you don't see it.

3 Use the creation tool to create your very own Memoji.

4 Tap **Done** in the top-right corner to save and use your new Memoji.

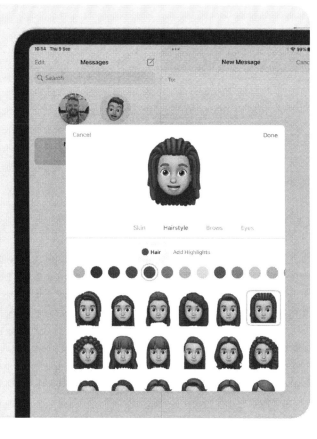

Delete a message

It's easy to delete an accidentally sent message: just **tap and hold** on the message, then choose **Undo Send**.

Once you've deleted a message, the other person will see a line of text that says "*{your name} unsent a message*", but they won't be able to see what the message originally said.

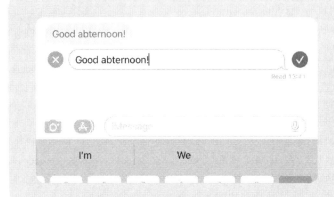

Edit a message

If you make a spelling mistake, get the time wrong, or simply say the wrong thing, then it's possible to edit a message that you've already said. To do this **tap and hold** on the message, then choose **Edit.** Next, make your changes, then tap the **tick** button. Once you've edited a message, the other person will see a line of text that says "*Edited*" below the message.

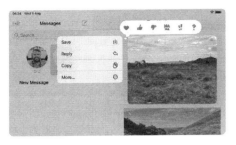

Add a Tapback sticker

If you want to add a personal touch to a delivered message, **tap and hold** on the message bubble to see six stickers that can be attached and seen by the recipient.

To see the details of a contact

Tap on their **name** or **image** at the top of the screen, then choose **Info**. On the following panel, tap on the **small arrow** at the top of the screen to see the recipients details.

Share your current location

Meeting a friend somewhere in town? If they're having trouble finding you, tap on their **name** at the top of the screen, choose **Info**, then tap the **Send My Location** button.

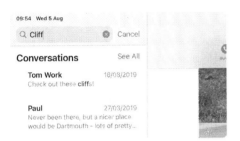

Search through messages

From the home screen of the Messages app, use the search field in the sidebar to find recent contacts, links, photos, and search through message content.

Delete messages

You can tell Messages to automatically remove chats after either 30 days or 1 year. To activate this feature, go to **Settings > Messages > Keep Messages**.

Keep audio messages

By default, audio messages are automatically deleted after 2 minutes. To keep them forever, go to **Settings > Messages**, then scroll down where you'll see an option for storing audio messages for longer.

Send a full-screen effect

Want to really grab someone's attention with a message? Try sending a full-screen effect. With the Messages app you can include one of nine effects that take over the screen for a brief moment. Here's how it works:

1 Compose your text, then instead of tapping the blue send arrow, **tap and hold** on it.

2 Tap the **Screen** tab at the top of the screen, then select an effect by swiping to across the screen with your finger.

3 Once you've found an effect tap the **blue arrow** button to send the message.

Send an emoji

To send an emoji, tap the **Emoji** button on the keyboard while composing a message. It's at the bottom of the screen next to the spacebar and microphone. You can swipe left and right to scroll through emoji's or tap the grey icons at the bottom of the screen to jump to an emoji category.

Send a handwritten note

Using the iPad's large display, you can write a handwritten note and send it using Messages. To do this tap the **handwriting** icon in the bottom-right corner of the keyboard, write your message, then tap Send. While handwriting a message you can also choose from a selection of preset messages by tapping the **timer** icon.

Automatically turn words into emoji's

So you've composed a message, but you want to liven it up with some fun emoji's. It's surprisingly easy, thanks to a clever feature that automatically scans your message for emoji-related words then lets you replace them with a tap. Here's how:

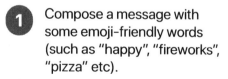

1 Compose a message with some emoji-friendly words (such as "happy", "fireworks", "pizza" etc).

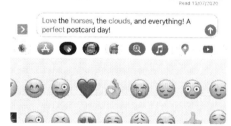

2 Tap the **emoji** button on the keyboard. Any emoji-friendly words will glow gold.

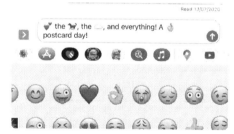

3 Tap on the gold words that you'd like to replace and they will automatically swap from text to emoji graphics.

85

Send a quick sketch

With the Messages app you can draw a message and send it with just a few taps of your finger. Here's how it works:

1 When you're viewing or replying to a message, tap the **Digital Touch** button above the keyboard. It looks like two fingertips over a heart.

2 Start to draw on the black panel in the lower area of the screen. You'll see your drawing come to life.

3 Once you've finished tap the **blue arrow** icon to send the drawing.

It's not just a drawing you can send, there are five other effects including a heart beat and a fireball:

Taps	**Fireball**	**Kiss**	**Heartbeat**	**Broken Heart**
Simply tap anywhere on the black panel and an animated tap will appear.	Press and hold on the screen with your finger. When you let go a fireball effect will be sent.	Tap with two fingers and you'll send a kiss message.	Tap and hold on the screen and an animated heartbeat will be sent.	Tap and hold with two fingers then slide downwards to send a broken heart.

Send a message with an animated effect

Four animated effects are included within the Messages app: a slam dunk, a loud shout, gentle whisper, or invisible ink. To send one of these effects:

1 Compose your message, then instead of tapping the blue send arrow, **tap and hold** on it.

2 In the pop-up window, tap one of the four options on the right-side of the screen to see a preview of how it looks.

3 Once you're happy with an effect, tap the **blue arrow** to send the message.

Manage your calendar

Learn how to add events and manage multiple calendars...

The calendar app on your iPad is surprisingly powerful. It can juggle multiple events throughout your day, factor in the time it takes to travel from one event to another, and even automatically block out chunks of time when you're on the road.

To find the Calendar app, simply search for it or look for this icon:

MON
24

The basics

1 Tap the **Calendars** button to toggle individual calendars on or off.

2 Tap the **Inbox** button to accept calendar event invites, and see the replies you've sent.

3 Tap the **sidebar** button to show or hide the sidebar.

4 By tapping the **plus** button, you can add a new event to the calendar. See across the page for more on this.

5 Toggle between day, week, month, and year views using these tabbed buttons.

6 Tap on the **search** button to look for a specific event, such as a birthday, hotel booking, or public holiday.

Add a calendar event

1. Tap the **plus** button in the top-left corner.

2. Give the event a name by tapping on the grey **Title** text.

3. If the event takes place at a location, then tap the grey **Location** text to search for a place. A list of recent locations will also be available for you to use.

4. Tap **Repeat** if you'd like the event to occur every day, week, bi-weekly, month, or year.

5. You can ask the Calendar app to automatically factor in travel time, then block out your calendar for the duration of the trip. To do this tap **Travel Time**, then toggle it on.

6. Tap **Invitees** to invite people to share the calendar event with you.

7. Tap the **Add** button when you're ready to add the event to your calendar.

If you're busy, use Day view

By using the Day view you can easily see detailed information for the day ahead. You can also jump from week to week by swiping through the days near the top of the screen.

Choose the default calendar

If you're the primary scheduler for a family or work calendar, then it's helpful to make that specific calendar the default choice. To do this go to **Settings** > **Calendar** > **Default Calendar**.

Get automatic alerts

If you'd like to be automatically reminded of birthdays and events before they happen, go to **Settings** > **Calendar** > **Default Alert Times**.

Tap for details

By tapping on an event you can easily delete it or view the location on a map.

Add an event with Siri

To quickly add an event to your calendar, initiate Siri then say something like *"add a calendar event to pick up Sam at 6 PM"*.

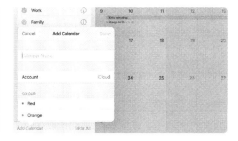

Add a new calendar

If you'd like to create a calendar for specific events, tap the **Calendars** button at the top of the screen then tap **Add Calendar**.

Make a FaceTime video call

Make a free video call to friends and family using FaceTime...

With FaceTime, you can be with friends and family at any time and place. Whether it's a birthday, anniversary, meeting, or just a chat, FaceTime lets you be a part of the moment with crystal clear video and audio.

FaceTime works over both Wi-Fi or a cellular connection, and enables you to call another iPad, iPhone, iPod touch, or a Mac. It works like a phone call, but it's free, supports video, and you can even add realtime visual effects.

You'll find the FaceTime app already installed on your iPad. To find it, just tap on this icon:

Sign in if you haven't used FaceTime before. You'll then see your contacts listed down the middle of the screen. Tap a contact to begin calling them, or alternatively tap **New FaceTime**, enter the contact in the **To:** field, then tap the **Phone** button to make a FaceTime audio call, or the **FaceTime** button to make a video call.

The basics

1 You can move the preview image of yourself around the screen by dragging it with your finger.

2 Tap the **Effects** button to apply a wide range of filters, shapes, and video effects.

3 Flip your camera around using this button to show what's behind your iPad.

4 Take a photo of the conversation using this white button. Keep in mind that the other person will see a message to let them you've taken a photo.

5 Tap this panel to access additional controls (see across page).

6 End the call using this button.

7 Send a message the person you're chatting too by tapping this button.

8 Toggle audio sources (see across page for more).

9 Mute your microphone using this button.

10 Turn off your camera.

Access additional controls

During a FaceTime call, tap the **upper panel** to invite more people (see below for further details), share a link, or silence any further join requests.

Swap to your headphones

If you have Bluetooth headphones connected to your iPad, then tap then **audio** button in the upper panel to swap the audio to your headphones.

Replace your face with an emoji

During the FaceTime call, tap the **Effects** button in the bottom-left corner. Tap on the **Animoji** icon, then select an existing avatar, or custom-made Memoji.

Make a group call

With support for up to 32 people at once, making a group FaceTime call is a great way to communicate with friends, family and work colleagues. Here's how it works:

1 Open the FaceTime app, then tap **New FaceTime**.

2 Enter the contacts you want to call in the **To:** field.

3 Tap the **Phone** button to make a FaceTime audio call, or the **FaceTime** button to make a video call.

4 If you would like to add an additional person during the call, tap the **participants** at the top of the screen and then tap **Add People**. Enter the contact's name, phone number or email address, then tap **Add People**. When someone is added to a Group FaceTime call, they can't be removed from the call. In order for that person to leave the call, they need to end the Group FaceTime call on their own device.

Tips for making a great FaceTime call:

✅ You can only FaceTime someone who has an iPhone, iPad, or Mac.

✅ Make sure the other person can see you. It's easy to forget where the camera is pointing, so use the small preview image to check your appearance.

✅ The microphone is located on the top of your iPad, so if the other person says they can't hear you, make sure your fingers aren't covering the bottom of the iPad.

✅ If you turn your iPad on its side during a call, the other person will see more of the room around you.

Take amazing photos

Get to know the camera app and all of its features...

The iPad might not be the first choice of camera for many, but that hasn't stopped millions of people from capturing magical moments and memories on the spot. The latest iPads continues that tradition, with a 12-megapixel camera that's capable of taking beautiful photos, can capture 4K video, and even film in slow motion. Additionally, the front-facing FaceTime camera is great for making video calls or taking a fun selfie.

Helping you to capture these moments is the Camera app. It's simple and intuitive to use, yet offers so many possibilities. To find the Camera app, just look for this icon:

The basics

1. Manually zoom in or out using the vertical slider on the left-side of the screen. On an iPad Pro tap the **1X** button instead.

2. Toggle Live Photo mode on or off by using this button.

3. Tap this button to set a timer.

4. If you have an iPad Pro, then tap this button to enable / disable the camera flash.

5. Swap between the front or back facing cameras.

6. Take a photo, or tap and hold to capture a Burst Mode photo.

7. Jump to your most recently taking photo by tapping this thumbnail image.

8. You can swap between camera modes by swiping or tapping the shortcut buttons here.

Tap to focus

The camera will automatically focus onto a prominent object or area of light, but if you need to manually focus the camera, just tap on the area or subject you wish to focus on. You'll see a yellow square flash below your finger to confirm that the camera has been focused on the area.

Lock the focus and aperture

To lock the focus and aperture, and keep it locked to that position, **tap and hold** on a subject or area. After a second or two a flashing yellow box beneath your finger will indicate that the camera focus has been locked.

Snap with the volume buttons

It's possible to take a photo by pressing the **volume up or down** buttons on the side of your iPad. This is especially useful for taking selfies with your arm outstretched.

Access from the lock screen

The quickest way to open the Camera app is via the lock screen of your iPad. To do this, just **swipe the Lock Screen from right-to-left** and the Camera viewfinder will appear.

Turn the flash on and off

To toggle the flash off, tap the **lightning** button on the right-side of the screen. You'll see options for activating the flash automatically, turning it on or off.

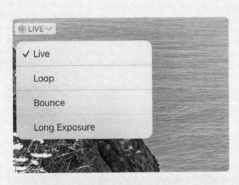

Live Photos explained

Whenever you take a photo, your iPad captures a few frames before and after the shot. By doing this it creates a short video of the moment that you can play back by **pressing and holding** on the photo when viewed in the Photos app. You'll know if a photo can be played back by a "LIVE" badge in the top-left corner. You can also tap this badge to enable three visual effects: Loop, Bounce, and Long Exposure.

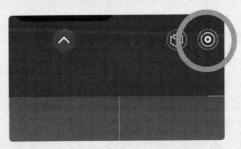

Turn Live Photos off

If you don't need (or like) the Live Photo feature, then you can disable it by tapping the **Live Photo** icon on the right-side of the screen.

Take a Portrait Photo with iPad Pro

Portrait photos are amazing. They mimic a DSLR camera by blurring the background behind a person. To do this your iPad Pro uses machine learning to automatically detect the face and hair of a subject, the distance between them and the background, then it blurs the background to create a beautiful 3D effect. To use Portrait mode:

1 Open the **Camera** app and select **Portrait** mode.

2 Place the subject at least 2 feet away. If they are too close the Camera app will let you know.

3 Tap the **capture** button to take the photo.

Use Portrait Lighting to take amazing selfies

By using Portrait Lighting mode you can simulate a number of professional photography effects and tools, such as a gold bounce card, to create even more beautiful looking photos. There are six effects to choose from:

Natural Light	**Studio Light**	**Contour Light**	**Stage Light**	**Stage Light Mono**	**High-Key Mono**
Your subject's face in sharp focus against a blurred background.	A clean look with your subject's face brightly lit.	Adds subtle shadows and highlights to the subject's face.	Your subject's face is spotlit against a deep black background.	Like Stage Light, but in black and white.	Adds a beautiful monochromatic effect.

To enable Portrait Lighting mode, open the **Camera** app and select **Portrait**. You'll see five buttons appear towards the bottom of the screen: Natural Light, Studio Light, Contour Light, Stage Light and Stage Light Mono. Select an effect by swiping through the options. Watch the screen to see the effect apply to your face in real-time. Press the **capture** button to take a photo.

You can choose another effect, even after the photo has been saved, by tapping the **Edit** button within the Photos app.

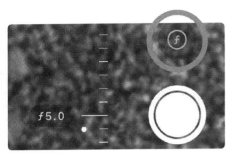

Adjust the portrait depth

While taking a portrait photo you can adjust how blurred the background is. To do this tap the (**f**) button on the right-side of the screen, then move the **Depth Control** slider up or down.

Disable Portrait mode effect

To disable the Portrait effect in a photo, open the image, tap **Edit**, then tap the yellow **Portrait** button at the top of the screen.

Shoot a video

Capturing video is easy, just swipe your finger across the camera viewfinder until **VIDEO** is centreed, then tap the **red** button.

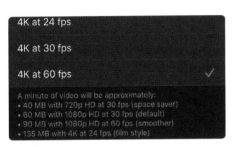

Enable 4K video recording

To enable 4K video recording, open the **Settings** app, tap **Camera**, then select **Record Video**. On the following panel you'll be able to enable video recording at 4K.

Slow motion video

One of the most fun camera features included with iPad is the ability to shoot video in slow motion at 240 frames per second. It's great for capturing fast-moving objects.

Film in slo-mo

While in the Camera app, swipe the text at the bottom of the screen until **SLO-MO** is centred. Next, tap the red record button to start filming your slow-motion video.

Edit a slow-mo video

To edit the slow-motion parts of a video, open the video in the **Photos** app, then tap the **Edit** button.

You'll notice a timeline at the bottom of the screen that's broken up by thin white lines. In the centre the lines are spaced further apart. This is the part of the clip which plays back in slow motion.

You can lengthen or shorten this slow motion part of the clip by dragging the white handles, then preview the clip by tapping the **play** button.

Capture a panoramic shot

Have you ever wanted to capture an incredibly beautiful vista? By using the PANO mode you can do just this by taking a super-wide, 180-degree photo.

PANO mode works by taking one very wide continuous photo. As you rotate on the spot, the camera captures the image as it appears on the right side of the lens. If there's any movement in front of you (such as people walking by), then you might see a few visual errors, but for vistas and still scenes the PANO mode works wonders.

1. Open the **Camera** app and select **PANO** mode.

2. You'll see a thumbnail in the centre of the screen with a white arrow pointing right.

3. Tap the **Camera** button at the bottom of the screen to start capturing a panoramic shot.

4. Slowly pan your device to the right. Keep a steady hand — if you wobble too much black bars will appear at the top and bottom of the photo.

5. Tap the **thumbnail** in the bottom corner to check out your panoramic image.

Capture time-lapse video

Have you ever wanted to capture a sun set, the changing tides, or the movement of clouds? Using the Camera app you can do this with the time-lapse feature. It works by capturing multiple photos, instead of video, over a period of time.

To capture a time-lapse video, open the **Camera** app, then select **TIME-LAPSE**. Next, place your iPad in a suitable location. Make sure it's steady – any movements over time will ruin the time-lapse effect. When you're ready, tap the **red record** button. Leave your iPad for a few moments or minutes - the longer the better as you'll capture more footage - then tap the red record button again to end the time-lapse.

How to use the Camera timer

To enable the timer, open the **Camera** app and look for a **timer** icon just above the photo button. Tap it and you'll see three text options appear: **Off**, **3s** and **10s**. These correspond to the timer settings, so off is the standard setting, 3s gives you three seconds to pose, and 10s gives you 10 seconds to prepare yourself. Tap whichever you need, then tap the **Camera** button to snap a photo. You'll see a countdown appear on-screen. After it has ended, your iPad will capture a photo and save it to your library.

Capture a burst mode photo

The Camera app comes with a feature called Burst Mode. It works by taking 10 photos every second, then saves them as a collection within the Photos app. It's particularly helpful if you're trying to take an action shot.

When you're ready to take a burst mode photo, **tap and hold** the **camera** button, then let go when you've captured the moment.

Select a burst mode favourite

Burst mode photos are saved as a stack in the Photos app, with a "favourite" image which represents the best moment from the lot. To select a new favourite and discard the others, open the stack, then tap the **Select** button at the top of the screen. A selection of thumbnails will appear along the bottom. Tap on your favourite then tap **Done**. You'll then be asked if you would like to keep the other photos or just the one you've favourited.

View and edit your Photos

Learn how to view, organise, and edit your photos...

The Photos app is a portal to your memories. Stored within its colourful icon are hundreds, if not thousands of treasured photos and videos. Photos of yapping dogs, family members, stunning landscapes, unflattering selfies, and treasured holidays. This is one of those apps that you're going to be opening on a day-to-day basis, so keep it somewhere prominent on the Home screen where you can quickly tap it.

Open the app, and you'll discover a clean, tidy interface that appears to be basic and easy to use. In many ways it is, but dig a little deeper, and you'll find one of the most productive and in-depth apps available for the iPad. With just one fingertip it's possible to edit photos, create albums, move and delete images, view memories, and much more.

The basics

1 Whenever you want to browse your photo libraries, albums, and media types, tap the **sidebar** icon in the top-right corner. If you don't see the icon then swipe inwards from the let side of the screen.

2 View your photo library as individual photos, or grouped by days, months, and years using these tabs at the top of the screen.

3 Select multiple photos using this button.

4 Tap the **options** button to zoom in or out, adjust the aspect ratio, filter photos, or view them on a map.

5 Tap and hold on a photo to copy it, select it, share it, favourite it, or delete it.

All Photos

When viewing **All Photos**, you'll see a nearly endless grid of photos scrolling upwards and off the screen. You can scroll through them and tap on an image to see it bigger, or you can pinch to zoom in or out to see your photos spread over a wider range of time.

Days

Tap on the **Days** tab and you'll see a beautiful grid of images representing a single day. The Photos app intelligently organises your images, hiding duplicates while selecting a highlighted image or video.

Months

The **Months** view organises the most meaningful events into groups, then displays them as individual cards in a scrollable panel. The app tries to intelligently select the best photo or video to remind you of what the event was about. Think of it as a greatest hit library of your memories.

Years

Years gives you a high-level overview of your photo library, but what makes this view really special is it's dynamic and based on context. So open the Years view on your birthday and you'll see photos from your birthday celebrations going back as far as your photo library extends.

Featured Photos

For You

Notice the **For You** option in the sidebar. Tap this and you'll be presented with albums of images that are organised into events, subjects, and highlights.

Every day a new set of albums and images will appear. Tap on an album to see more photos, the date they were taken, where they were taken, and related albums.

Albums

Scroll down the sidebar and you'll see a collection of albums called **My Albums**. These are based on:

*   Albums you've created
*   People and places
*   Videos and selfies
*   Live Photos and Portrait Photos
*   Panoramas
*   Time-lapse videos and slo-mo videos
*   Burst mode photos
*   Screen recordings
*   Animated photos
*   RAW images from a DSLR or iPhone Pro

Create an album

To create a new album, tap on **All Albums** in the sidebar, tap the blue **plus** icon at the top of the screen, then choose **New Album**. Enter a title for the album then tap the **Save** button.

A window will then appear displaying all of the photos on your iPad. Tap the images you'd like to add to the new Album, then tap **Done** to save the new album.

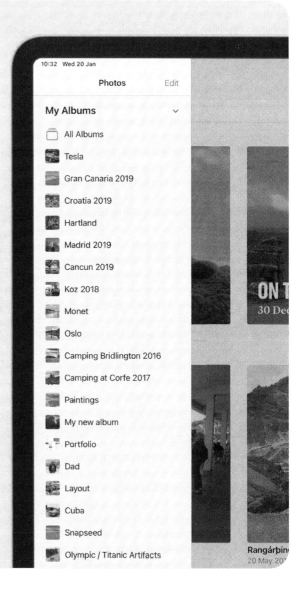

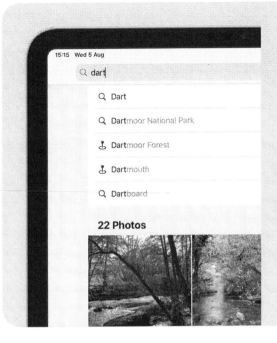

Search your photos

The Photos app can recognise objects, faces and locations, then automatically organise groups of images into albums. This clever form of visual recognition has another benefit: intelligent searching. To search for something in an image, tap the **Search** button in the sidebar.

Search for *"California"* and you'll see all your photos of California. You can be even more specific. So search for *"Trees in California"* and the Photos app will automatically show photos of trees within California. You can try other queries such as *"Tom eating pizza"*, or *"Sarah riding a horse"* and the Photos app will instantly present you with the correct results.

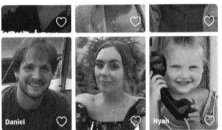

People and Places

After scanning every photo in your library to look for photos of locations and faces, the Photos app collates them into the **People and Places** section of the Photos app.

Find People and Places

To see these images just open the sidebar then tap either **People** or **Places**.

Check out the places view

Tap on the **Places** option in the sidebar, and you'll see a map view with all of your photos placed in the correct location.

Watch a video of someone

To watch a video of someone in the People album, select them then tap the **play** button near the top of the screen.

Add a name to a person

To add a name to someone in the People album, tap the **+ Add Name** field at the top of the screen.

Add someone to Favourites

If you like to regularly see the photos of a family member or friend, tap the small **heart** icon in the bottom corner of their thumbnail image.

Get information about a photo

Open an image, then tap the **info (i)** button in the upper-right corner of the screen. You will then see a pop-up panel full of information, including a map of where the photo was taken.

Favourite an image

Tap the **heart** button at the top of the screen and the image will be added to the Favourites album - accessible from the sidebar.

Delete a photo

While viewing an image tap the blue **Trash** button in the top-right corner of the screen.

The basics of editing a photo

To improve the look of a photo you've taken on your iPad, select an image in the Photos app, then tap the **Edit** button in the top-right corner. You'll see the screen darken, and a number of editing tools appear:

1 Tap the **ellipse** button to add markup to an image.

2 Tap **Done** when you're finished editing an image.

3 While editing a photo, tap the wand button to automatically improve the look of an image.

4 Tap the **Live Photo** button to disable the live effect, choose a different Live Photo still, or to mute the Live Photo footage.

5 Tap the **Adjustment Tools** button to access the various editing tools.

6 Choose from a variety of photo filters.

7 Crop and rotate an image by tapping this button.

8 Select and work with editing tool by scrolling through this horizontal list.

101

Fine tune an image

Below the wand tool on the right-side of the screen are various tools for adjusting a photos exposure, brilliance, highlights, shadows, contrast, brightness, black point, saturation, colour, warmth, tint, sharpness, noise, and vignette.

You can swipe vertically through these tools to explore them, and then tap on one to select it.

To make fine adjustments with a tool, use the vertical slider on the right-side of the screen.

By experimenting with each tool, you'll discover your own favourite settings and adjustments.

Trim and edit videos

Open a video, tap the **Edit** button, and you'll find the same image editing tools that we discussed on the previous page. All of these tools enable you to adjust the light and colour of a video, rotate or crop it, and even add filters.

You can also trim the beginning and end of a video to adjust its timing and length. To do this, tap **Edit** then make a note of the timeline which appears just above the editing tools. By dragging the handles on each side of the timeline you can adjust the start and end points of the video.

Hide photos

If you'd like to hide a photo from the Photos, Memories and Shared albums, open the photo, tap the **options** button in the upper-corner, then tap **Hide**.

The photo will now be copied to a new **Hidden** album. This folder is locked, and can only be opened with Face or Touch ID. Additionally, if you would like to also hide the Hidden folder entirely, then open the **Settings** app, tap **Photos**, scroll down, the un-toggle the **Hidden Album** option.

Transfer photos from a camera

How to move photos from a traditional camera to your iPad...

While the iPad can take amazing photos, it still can't match the quality or resolution of a traditional camera or DSLR. Copying photos from a traditional camera to your iPad is a fairly simple task, but before you get started, you'll need an adapter to enable your camera or its SD card to talk to your iPad. There are two available, one for the traditional iPad and iPad mini, and another for the iPad Pro or iPad Air:

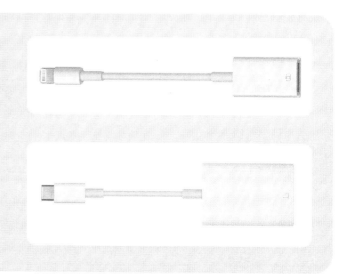

Lightning to USB adapter

Used to connect your camera to an iPad or iPad mini via a USB cable. It's available from the Apple Store.

USB-C to SD card reader

You can use this adapter to plug an SD card directly into your iPad Pro or iPad Air. It works with UHS-II SD cards and is backwards compatible with other SD cards and adapters. Also available from the Apple Store.

If using the Lightning to USB camera adapter

1. Use the USB cable that came with your camera to connect the camera to the camera adapter.

2. Turn on the camera and make sure it's in transfer mode. If you need help with this step, see the camera's manual.

3. Open **Photos** on your iPad, then tap **Import**.

4. Select the photos and videos you want to import, then select your import destination:
   - Import all photos on the camera: Tap **Import All**.
   - Import just some photos: Tap the photos you want to import (a checkmark appears for each), tap **Import**, then tap **Import Selected**.

5. After the photos and videos have been imported, disconnect the camera adapter.

If using the USB-C to SD card reader

1. Remove the SD card from your camera. It's usually located underneath a plastic flap, and you will need to push down on the SD card to release it.

2. Insert the SD card into the card reader adapter.

3. Open **Photos** on your iPad, then tap **Import**.

4. Select the photos and videos you want to import, then select your import destination:
   - Import all photos on the camera: Tap **Import All**.
   - Import just some photos: Tap the photos you want to import (a checkmark appears for each), tap **Import**, then tap **Import Selected**.

5. After the photos and videos have been imported, disconnect the SD card and place it back in your camera.

Transfer photos from a PC

Learn how to transfer photos saved on your PC to an iPad...

Using your iPad to view treasured photos is a great way to relive memories, thanks to its pin-sharp colourful display, and ability to automatically organise photos using date, location, and even the people within them. If you have a large number of photos on your PC and would like to transfer them to your iPad, then there are a number of ways to go about this...

Via iCloud

By using iCloud, not only do you store all of your images safely in the cloud, but you can also sync them across all of your devices, including a PC. The easiest way to import all of your photos to iCloud is to use the iCloud app. Here's how it works:

1 Visit the Microsoft Store, search for **iCloud**, then install it on your PC. Once installed, log in with the same Apple ID used for your iPad.

2 Using the iCloud app on your PC, make sure **Photos** is enabled by checking the tick box. Next, click **Options**, enable **iCloud Photos**, click **Done**, then click **Apply**.

3 Over on your iPad, be patient and wait for your PC to upload its photos to iCloud. After a while, they will begin to appear on your iPad.

Via FoneTrans for PC

This helpful piece of software is available from www.aiseesoft.com, and is able to transfer photos, music, contacts and more between your PC and iPad.

1 Install FoneTrans, then connect your iPad to your PC with a USB cable.

2 Once your iPad is recognised, click **Photos** in the sidebar, then choose **Photo Library**.

3 Click the **(+)** button, then choose **Add File** or **Add Folder**. Next, browse to where the photos are stored on your PC, select them, then click **Open**. Wait for your photos to be transferred to your iPad, then click **Close**. You will now find the imported images in the Photos app.

Listen to Music

Listen to your favourite tracks and albums on Apple Music...

The Music app has always been the best way to listen to music on iPad. It has a beautiful interface, access to millions of tracks via Apple Music, exclusive TV shows, curated playlists, videos, top charts, and Beats 1 Radio.

There's a limitless source of music available in Apple Music, but it comes at a price: to access the full service you'll need to pay a monthly subscription. It's priced slightly differently for each country but roughly works out about the same as a large takeaway pizza. For anyone who listens to the latest charts, streams music on a daily basis or has a wide variety of music tastes, it's definitely worth the asking price. For everyone else, Apple Music still offers Apple Music 1, the ability to follow artists and preview music.

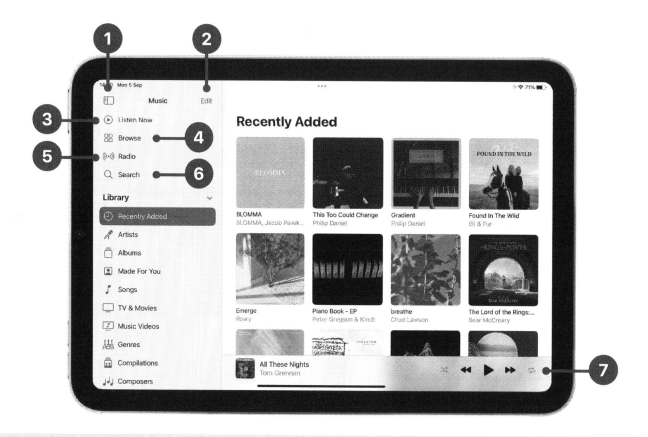

The basics

1 Use the sidebar to navigate through your library and explore Apple Music.

2 Tap **Edit** to remove genres of music from your Library, or to re-order items.

3 Tap **Listen Now** to see playlists created by Apple which suit your tastes, your listening history, what friends are listening to, and new releases.

4 Tap **Browse** and you'll find the latest tracks, top charts, music videos, and TV shows exclusive to Apple Music.

5 Tap **Radio** to discover a wide range of radio stations for every taste.

6 Tap **Search** to find songs, albums, artists, or lyrics. Either saved on your iPad or on Apple Music.

7 While a song is playing, tap on this panel to access playback controls.

Music

Play and download 60 million songs.

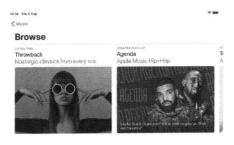

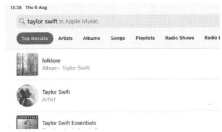

Sign up for Apple Music

Without an Apple Music subscription you can only listen to 30-second preview clips. You can sign up for a monthly subscription through the app. Alternatively, open the iTunes app to purchase music without a subscription.

Explore Apple Music

Once subscribed, you'll find literally millions of tracks, albums, playlists, radio stations, and music videos within Apple Music. Tap on the **Browse** button towards the top of the sidebar.

Search for music

If you're looking for an artist, song, album, or even lyrics, then tap the **Search** button in the sidebar. You can use the tabs near the top of the screen to search through both Apple Music and your library.

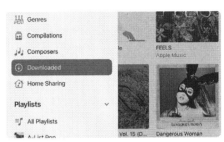

Add music to your Library

If there's a track or album that you'd like to save to your Library, tap the **+Add** button at the top of the screen.

Download new music

To automatically download music to your iPad whenever you add a new album or track, open the **Settings** app, tap **Music** then toggle **Automatic Downloads** on.

Browse your offline music

If you don't have a signal and need to play music that's saved to your iPad, open the sidebar then choose **Downloaded**.

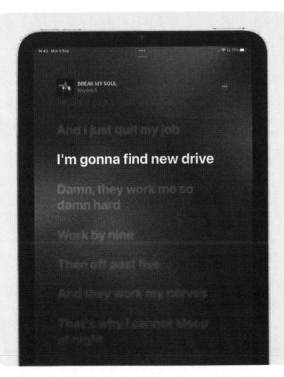

View music lyrics

Have you ever struggled to understand the lyrics of a song as it plays in the background? Using the Music app you see fullscreen lyrics for all your favourite songs, similar to karaoke.

When listening to a song, tap on playback control panel at the bottom of the screen, then tap the lyrics button in the bottom-right corner of the screen. It looks like a small speech bubble. You'll then see a fullscreen lyrics view take over. If you don't see the **lyrics** button, just make sure you're looking at the music playback window. You can get to it at any moment by opening the Music app then tapping on the small album artwork thumbnail at the bottom of the screen.

Shuffle music

If you're bored of an album track order, tap **Shuffle** and you'll never know what song is coming up next.

Create a Playlist

To create a new playlist of your own, open the sidebar, scroll all the way down, then tap **New Playlist**.

Add to an existing playlist

If you'd like to add a track or album to an existing playlist, **tap and hold** on the track then choose **Add to a Playlist...** in the Share sheet.

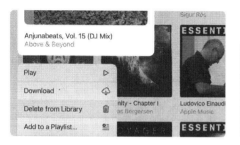

Delete a track or album

Fed up with a song or album? Just **tap and hold** on the track name or album artwork, then tap **Delete from Library**.

Like music to improve your recommendations list

Whenever you hear a great track or album, tap the **options** button in the corner of the screen (it looks like three dots) then tap the **Love** button. This tells Apple Music what genre of music you like. Keep doing this and over time the For You playlists and recommendations will get more and more accurate to your tastes in music.

Add a Music widget

By adding a Music widget to the Home Screen you can quickly jump to a recent song or album.

1. On the Home Screen, **tap and hold** in an empty part of the screen.

2. When all the apps start to wiggle, tap the **plus (+)** icon in the top-left corner.

3. Scroll down, then tap on **Music**. Select a widget size, then tap **+ Add Widget**.

Play similar music

If you're listening to a style of music and don't want it to end, then your iPad can automatically look for similar tracks and albums after the current one has finished.

1. While listening to music, tap the **list** button (≡) in the lower corner.

2. Next, tap the **loop** button (∞) which appears near the top of the screen.

3. Your iPad will automatically look for similar music.

Radio stations

Tap **Radio** in the sidebar to listen to Apple Music 1, radio stations from around the country, plus bespoke stations that are automatically compiled around your listening history.

Check out music videos

To browse the latest music videos, open the sidebar, tap **Browse**, scroll down then tap **Music Videos**.

See the top charts

What to see what's number one in the charts? Open the sidebar, tap **Browse**, then tap **Top Charts**.

Sing along to your favourite song with Apple Music Sing

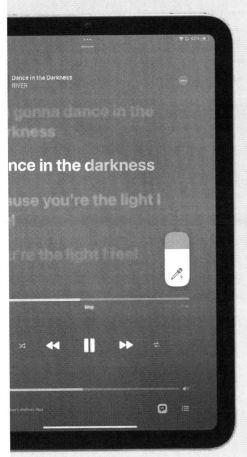

With Apple Music Sing, you can sing along to your favourite songs with adjustable vocals and real-time lyrics. Using an on-screen lyric slider, you can decide whether to sing with the original artist vocals or take the lead, and there are millions of songs to try out. Here's how it works:

1 Open the Music app, tap **Search**, then choose **Sing**. You can then explore the many tracks and playlists available for you to sing along to. Alternatively, try opening your favourite song and keep your fingers crossed that it supports Apple Music Sing.

2 After a song begins to play, tap the controls near the bottom of the screen to show the song full screen.

3 Tap the **lyrics** button in the bottom-left corner of the screen. It looks like a small speech bubble

4 Tap the **Apple Music Sing** button in the lower-right corner of the screen. It looks like a microphone with stars around it. If the Sing button isn't available, the song doesn't support this feature.

5 To follow along with the song, singout loud words as they glow white. To jump forwards or backwards through the song, scroll through the lyrics and tap on the section you want to replay.

6 To reveal the playback controls, tap near the bottom of the screen. You can then disable Apple Music Sing, jump to another track, or control the playback.

Watch TV & Movies

Never miss an episode of your favourite show with this helpful app...

With so many sources of video content, subscription services, and streaming neworks, it has become difficult to keep track of the latest episodes of your favorite TV shows. Thankfully, the Apple TV app for iPad makes it a little bit easier, by collating many of the latest releases into one app. It also houses any TV shows or movies which you've purchased on iTunes, and remembers where you last left off.

To find the Apple TV app on your iPad, just search for it using Spotlight, or look for this icon:

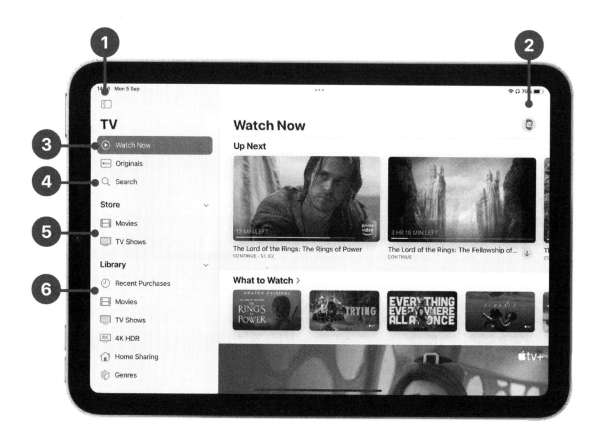

The basics

1 Use the sidebar to explore Apple TV and the content you've purchased.

2 Tap on your **profile photo** to manage subscriptions, redeem a Gift Card, or sign out.

3 If you're looking for inspiration, tap **Watch Now** to find suggested TV shows and movies.

4 It's pretty obvious, but by tapping **Search** you can look for movies, TV shows, or cast and crew.

5 Purchase a movie, TV show, or entire season by exploring these two options.

6 You'll find all of your purchases in the **Library** section of the app, split into TV Shows and Movies.

Toggle audio and subtitles

While watching a video, tap the **speech** icon next to the playback timer to toggle different audio sources or subtitles.

Access special features

If you've rented or purchased a movie with special features, then watch the movie in landscape mode. You'll see buttons for special features appear along the bottom of the screen.

Action & Adventure · 2017 2 hrs 13 min

Spider-Man [Tom Holland] begins to navigate his new identity as the web-slinging super hero under the watchful eye of his mentor Tony Stark.

▶ Play

Download a film to your iPad

If you want to save a purchased film to your iPad, tap on its **artwork**, then tap the **iCloud** button.

Learn more about cast & crew

Search for an actor, producer, director, or other member of crew, and you can see what films they've been in, created, or made a guest appearance.

Add something to Up Next

If you discover a movie or show that you'd like to watch later, tap the **+ Plus** button in the top-right corner to add it to your Up Next list. To find this list, tap **Watch Now** then look for the Up Next panel at the top of the screen.

Take part in a workout class

Try yoga, dance, and core exercises...

Fitness+ is a new subscription service from Apple, focused on workout classes that you can do from home. It's rather like a VHS/DVD workout tape, but because Fitness+ combines both your iPad and Apple Watch, you can see your progress and heart rate in realtime. New classes are added daily too, so there's always something new to try.

Fitness+ offers 10 different workouts types, including: High Intensity Interval Training (HIIT), Strength, Yoga, Dance, Core, Cycling, Treadmill (for running and walking), Rowing, and Mindful Cooldown. The service also learns what you like, and monitors your progress, then recommends workouts based on what you enjoy doing.

To find the Fitness+ service, open the Fitness app on your iPad. Its app icon looks like this:

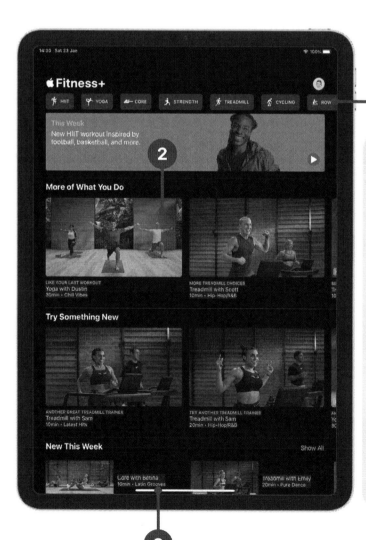

The basics

After opening the Fitness app, you'll see an overview of the classes available, with shortcuts along the top of screen for categories of workouts.

1. These are the 10 workout types offered by Fitness+. You can scroll through them going right to left. Tap on one to see which classes are available.

2. These classes are based on your recent activity. After taking part in a few classes, you'll see accurate suggestions that are designed to push you further.

3. Scroll down to find a selection of beginner classes, where you can learn the basics of yoga, strength training, and more.

Use an Apple Watch

Fitness+ works best if you're wearing an Apple Watch. This allows the app to track your heart rate and movements, with two benefits:

1 You can accurately track your calories as the class progresses. These will appear both on your Apple Watch, and on your iPad.

2 You can pause and play the class using your Apple Watch.

Pick a class

After finding a class on the Fitness+ screen, tap on it to find out more. You'll see how long the class lasts, can take a look at a short preview, begin the class, and see what music tracks are used in the background.

Yoga with Jessica

Take part in a class

Once you begin a class, you'll see a trainer appear on-screen alongside two assistants. As the class progresses, you'll see your heart rate and total calories appear in the top-left corner. Over in the right corner, you'll see your fitness activity rings for the entire day so far. Watch as they slowly close during the class. If you decide to end a class early, tap on the screen then tap the **pause** button, or use your Apple Watch.

Use Maps to navigate the world

Discover new places, get route guidance, and more...

With a map of the entire globe in your iPad, it's no longer possible to get lost in a busy city or strange new land. That's exactly what the Maps app gives you, alongside directions, real-time traffic information, transit timetables, 3D views of major cities and more. All of this for free and fully accessible at any time.

To find the Map app, just unlock your iPad then tap on this icon:

The basics

1 Tap on the **search field** to search for a place, address, or landmark.

2 Tap the **layers** button to swap view modes (see across page for more).

3 Tap the **compass arrow** button to move the map to your current location. Tap it for a second time and the map will rotate to match the orientation of your iPad.

4 This blue dot represents your current location in the world.

5 This is the main map view. You can pan and zoom using your fingers.

6 Notice the information panel on the side of the screen. This automatically displays your recent activity, so you might see how long it will take to get home, where your car is parked, or where an event in your calendar is happening. You'll also find any collections of places you've saved alongside recently viewed locations.

Swap view modes

When you open the Maps app, you'll see the world in a colourful vector mode that makes finding locations and landmarks easy. If you'd rather view the world using satallite imagery, see public transport details, or use the driving view, tap tap the **layers** button in the top right corner, then make a choice using the four options.

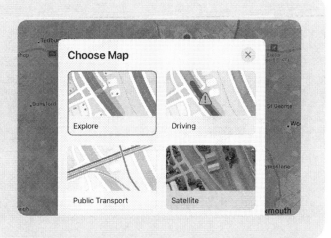

Drop a pin to find out more

To see detailed information about a specific point, simply **tap and hold** your finger on the screen and a pin will be dropped underneath it.

Share a location

Want to send an address to friends and family? Just search for the location, tap the options button, then choose **Share**.

Search Maps using Siri

If you'd rather search for a place using Siri, hold down the **Home** button on a regular iPad, or the **Power** button on iPad Pro or Air, wait for Siri to appear, then say something like "*where is the nearest hotel?*"

Explore what's nearby

To find local business and places of interest, tap on the **search** field in the upper-left corner, then use the various icons to see what's nearby. Scroll down, and you'll also find articles and guides to nearby cities.

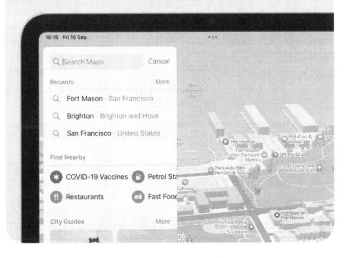

Call a business or place of interest

If you're exploring the map and find a local business or place of interest, tap on it to find out more. You might see TripAdvisor reviews, photos, opening times, phone numbers, and useful pieces of information.

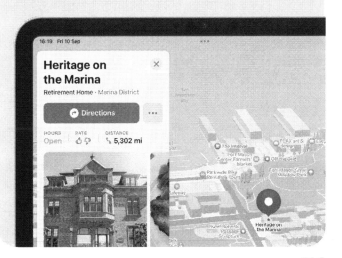

See a 3D map

Using the Maps app it's possible to navigate the world's most famous cities in beautiful 3D graphics. To view the 3D map, ensure you're in satellite mode, then zoom in on the map. When you're close to the ground, you'll notice a **3D** button appear in the upper-right corner. Tap it and the Maps view will tilt, then load a 3D landscape with detailed 3D buildings.

To rotate the image, place two fingers on the screen then rotate them. To tilt the camera, simultaneously move two fingers up or down the screen. Moving them left or right will pan the camera.

Look Around in first-person

Look Around mode lets you explore the world at street level using 360-degree imagery. It's almost like you're walking down the street itself.

To use the Look Around mode, zoom the map until you see a binocular icon appear in the bottom-right corner. At the time of writing, it will only appear in major cities within the United States. Once you see it, tap the icon and Look Around mode will begin.

To pan the view, just push it with your finger. To move in any direction, double tap where you want to go. You can also tap on a tag to see more information about the place or business.

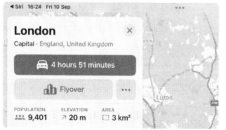

Enjoy a flyover tour

Want to enjoy a 3D tour of a city? Simply search for the city's name, then tap the **Flyover** button in the sidebar.

Search indoor maps with "Look Inside"

With the Maps app you can find your way around airports and shopping centres using the indoor maps feature, which displays the locations of stores, toilets, and more. Most international airports and major shopping centres are fully mapped. Just look for a "Look Inside" badge that appears beneath the name of the airport. When you see it, tap **Look Inside** to start exploring.

Turn-by-turn navigation

Satellite navigation and GPS technology have made driving to unfamiliar locations so much easier; and with an iPad, you can take advantage of this same technology to explore and navigate the world. It's wonderfully easy to use. Once set up, Maps will display the route in 3D, with road signs and written directions. And if the traffic conditions change, Maps will offer an alternative route for you to take.

1 To get started, open Maps then tap the **Search** field in the information panel. Next, enter the destination you wish the navigate to. This can be an address, zip code, or you can tap and hold on the map to drop a pin.

2 Once you've searched for an address, tap the blue **Directions** button to enable turn-by-turn instructions. Maps will automatically find the optimal route to the destination. It will also offer alternative routes, if any are available, which appear as opaque blue lines on the map. You can tap on these alternative routes to choose them.

3 Once you've found a suitable route tap the green **GO** button to begin following turn-by-turn directions.

Maps will automatically speak directions out-loud when you approach turns, lane changes, and exits - just as you'd expect if using a dedicated Sat-Nav device. You can even press the **Power** button to turn off your iPad display and it will light up whenever a change in direction is needed.

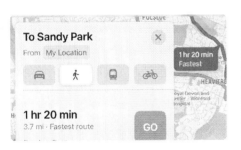

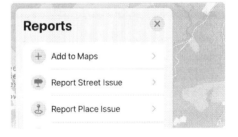

Walking or cycling directions

If you're planning a route on foot or a bike, then use the small graphical buttons to select either walking or cycling directions. If going by bike, then you can plan a route that avoids hills and busy roads. If you're wearing an Apple Watch, then you'll also receive haptic notifications when it's time to turn or change direction.

Set custom preferences

You can customise the Maps app to avoid tolls and motorways, automatically generate walking, cycling, or transport directions, and more. To do this, tap on your **profile photo** at the top of the information panel, then tap **Preferences**.

Report an issue with the map

To report an error or missing place, tap on your **profile photo** at the top of the information panel, then tap **Report an Issue**. You can then report on an issue with a place or route, or add something to maps such as an address, street, or cycle path.

Create, edit, and share Notes

Learn how to quickly jot down notes, plus much more...

At first glance, the Notes app is a fairly basic way to jot down ideas and lists. It's much more than that, however. With the Notes app you can collaborate with friends, draw and annotate, scan documents, format text, create tables, and more.

To find the Notes app, just look for this icon on the home screen of your iPad:

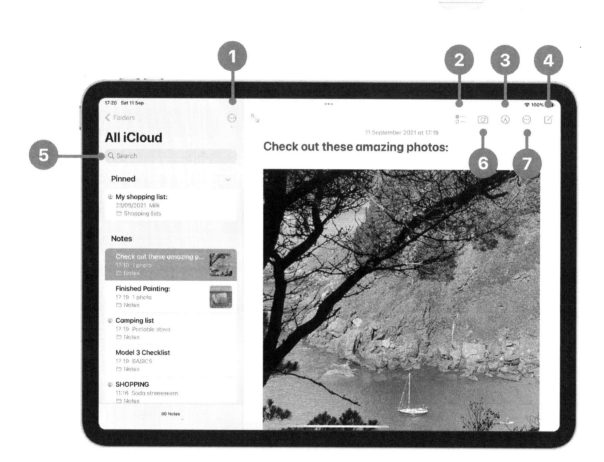

The basics

1 Tap the **options** button in the sidebar to toggle views, select multiple notes, or view attachments.

2 Create a checklist of items by tapping the **tick** icon.

3 Add a hand-drawn sketch to a note by tapping the **pencil** button.

4 Create a new note by tapping this button.

5 You can search for notes, words, and attachments by tapping on the **search** field.

6 Tap the **camera** button to attach a photo within a note. You can also scan documents using this button (turn over the page for more on this).

7 While viewing a note, tap the **options** button in the top-right corner to share it, move the note, add a grid background, or delete it.

11 September 2021 at 17:19

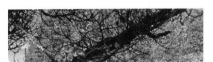

e amazing photos:

Create a new note

To create a new Note, open the **Notes** app, then tap the **New Note** button in the top-right corner.

Sketch a note

If you'd like to draw into a note, tap the **pencil** button in the top-right corner. A sketchpad will now appear on-screen, enabling you to draw with a pen, felt tip or pencil.

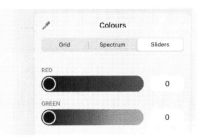

Change the line colour

You can change the colour of the line by tapping the **colour wheel**. A pop-up window will then appear enabling you to select colours from a grid, spectrum, or set of sliders.

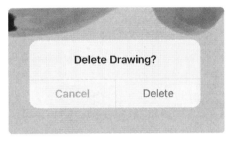

Delete a drawing

To quickly remove a sketch, tap ahead of it to insert the text input line, then tap the **delete** key on the keyboard.

View thumbnails of your notes

If you'd rather see thumbnail images of each note, rather than a list, tap on the **options** button in the sidebar, then choose **View as Gallery**.

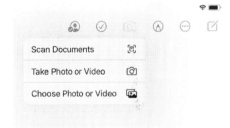

Insert a photo

To add a photo to a note, just tap the **camera** icon at the top of the screen, then select either **Take Photo or Video**, or **Choose Photo or Video**.

Create a table

Start by creating or opening a note, tap where you want to insert the table, then tap the **table** icon just above the keyboard. You'll then see a 2-by-2 table appear.

To add content to a row or column, tap on it then use the keyboard to enter text. To add additional rows or columns, tap the buttons above or to the left of the table.

Share a note

To send a note to someone else, tap the **options** button at the top of the screen, then tap **Send a Copy**.

Print a note

While viewing a note, tap the **options** button at the top of the screen, then choose **Print**. If you have a wireless printer that supports AirPrint, then it should appear in the Printer list.

Delete a note

From the overview screen of the Notes app, **tap and hold** on the note you wish to remove, then tap **Delete**. You can also swipe across a note in the sidebar then tap the **Delete** button.

Collaborate on a note

If you'd like to share and collaborate on a note with friends and family then it's an easy process on the iPad. If you're the creator of the note then it's yours to share, meaning you can invite others, see changes happen in real-time, and remove access to anyone that you've invited. Here's how it works:

1 Select the note that you would like to share, tap the **options** button at the top of the screen, then choose **Share Note.**

2 Use the Share panel to invite others from your Contacts book. You can also send invites via Message, Mail, Twitter and more.

3 Anyone invited will receive an iCloud link to open your note.

4 As they make changes to the note you'll see them appear in real-time with a yellow highlight that fades away after a moment. Your changes will appear with a purple highlight.

5 To remove someone's permission, tap the **Collaborate** button at the top of the screen, tap the person's name then choose **Remove Access**.

6 If you're tired of seeing notifications everytime someone makes a change, tap the **Collaborate** then un-toggle **Highlight All Changes**.

Search for a note

To find a specific note, open the sidebar then tap on the **search** field. You can search for keywords or use the suggestions below to filter note types.

Add a grid background

You can add a variety of grid-based backgrounds to a note. To do this tap the **options** button, then select **Lines & Grids**. On the following panel you can choose a style.

Pin a note

While viewing a note, tap the **options** button in the top corner then choose **Pin**. The note will then be pinned at the top of the overview screen, making it easier to find.

Scan a document

Using the notes app, it's possible to scan letters and documents, then attach them directly to a note. What's great is that scans actually look like scanned documents, thanks to some clever post-processing which straightens the image and fixes any white balance issues. To scan a document:

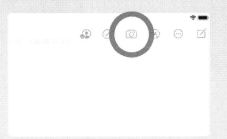

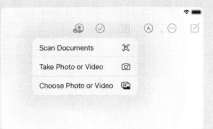

1 While viewing a note, tap the **camera** icon at the top of the screen.

2 Select the **Scan Documents** option.

3 When the camera view appears, move it over the document you wish to scan and your iPad will automatically recognise it.

4 Tap **Keep Scan** to save the image. You can continue to scan further documents, or tap **Save** to attach the image/s to your notes.

5 The scan will now be attached to your note as an image.

Create your own Siri Shortcuts

Create complex actions then perform them using just your voice...

Think of Siri Shortcuts as an app that lets you create complex tasks and actions, then invoke them by asking Siri. You can do things like ask Siri "where's my next appointment" and the digital assistant will give you instant directions to the next event in your calendar. Similarly, you might say "turn today's photos into a collage", and Siri will automatically grab any photos from the day and turn them into a beautiful collage.

To find the Siri Shortcuts app, ask Siri to open it or look for this icon on the Home Screen:

The basics

1 Tap **Select** to select, delete, or duplicate shortcuts.

2 If you've created a large number of shortcuts, then use the search bar to quickly find one.

3 You can use the sidebar to jump between your shortcuts, a gallery of pre-made shortcuts, and automated actions.

4 Tap the **plus** button to quickly create a brand new shortcut.

5 To discover a massive amount of Siri shortcuts tap the **Gallery** button. You'll discover shortcuts based around accessibility, the home, daily routines and much more.

6 Tap the **Automation** button to create an action that automatically runs at a certain time, place, event, or setting change.

7 Access your existing shortcuts here. You can also **tap and hold** on a shortcut to rename it, duplicate it, see more details or delete it.

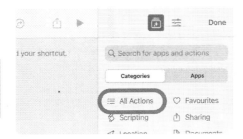
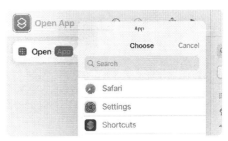

Create a new shortcut

Let's create a new Siri shortcut that instantly opens Safari then goes to the Apple homepage. Start by tapping the **plus (+)** button in the upper-left corner.

Add an Action

You'll see a selection of suggested actions and shortcuts in the panel on the right-side of the screen. Tap the action called **Open App**.

Select Safari

The next step is to select an app. Let's choose Safari. To do this, tap on the faint blue "App" text near the top of the screen. Next, scroll through the list of apps on your iPad and choose **Safari**.

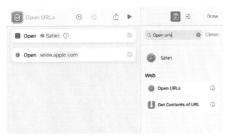
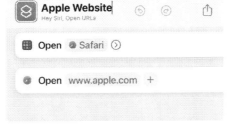
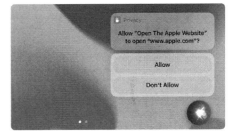

Enter an URL

We now want to jump straight to the Apple website. Use the search bar in the panel on the right side of the screen to look for **"Open URLs"**. Select this action, then tap the faint blue **URL** button. Next, type **www.apple.com.**

Give the shortcut a Siri name

We now need to give the shortcut a name. You'll use this name when invoking the shortcut using Siri. Tap on the **Shortcut Name** field at the top of the screen, then enter **Open The Apple Website**. Tap the **Done** button in the top-right corner to save this new shortcut.

Invoke your new shortcut

You're now ready to test your new shortcut. Hold down the **power** button to access Siri, then say out loud "open the Apple website". With a bit of luck, Safari should instantly open and take you to Apple's site.

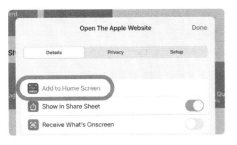

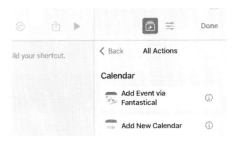

Add a Home Screen Shortcut

From the Siri Shortcuts home screen, **tap and hold** on a shortcut then tap the **Details** button. On the following screen tap **Add to Home Screen** double check everything looks good then tap **Add**.

Add a Shortcut Share Sheet

If you'd like to regularly invoke a Shortcut then adding it to the Share Sheet is a good idea. To do this **tap and hold** on a shortcut then tap the **Details** button. On the following screen toggle **Show in Share Sheet**.

Explore more actions

The Shortcuts app is packed with useful and interesting actions. If you'd like to explore them all, create a new action then tap **All Actions** in the sidebar. You can then scroll through the hundreds of available actions.

Create Reminders

Set yourself reminders so you'll never forget a thing...

The iPad already includes a notes app that can be used to jot down ideas and thoughts, but Reminders makes it easy to create to-do lists, set deadlines, and organise your life. It can also remind you with alerts at pre-determined times.

That's not all the app does, of course. It can group reminders into categories and even automatically sync reminders across all your devices via iCloud. To find the Reminders app, use Spotlight, or look for this icon:

The basics

1 Search for reminders, lists, or list items using the search bar at the top of the screen.

2 You can rearrange or delete entire lists by tapping the **Edit** button.

3 Select a reminder or list here. You can also rearrange items by tapping, holding, then dragging.

4 You can quickly add additional items to a reminder list by pressing the **Enter** key.

5 To create a brand new reminder list, tap the **Add List** button in the bottom-left corner.

Create a new Reminder

From the home screen of the Reminders app, tap the **Reminders** option under My Lists, then tap **New Reminder** in the bottom corner. Give it a name, then tap **Done**.

Remind on a date and time

To remind yourself to do something at a specific date and time, tap on the new reminder, then tap the **i** button. In the pop-up window, toggle **Date** and **Time** on, then set a day and specific time if necessary.

Remind yourself at a location

Similarly, you can also remind yourself when you reach a location. To do this toggle **Location**, then either enter an address or choose from one of the suggested options.

Share a reminder

Tap on the Reminder then tap the **options** button in the top-right corner. In the pop-up window you'll see an option called **Share List**. Tap this and you'll be able to send the reminder to someone you know.

Create a subtask

You can add a subtask to more complex reminders or lists. To do this tap on the reminder, tap the **i** button, then scroll down and choose **Subtasks**. Tap on it and then hit **Add Reminder** to add a subtask.

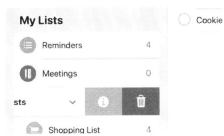

Create a group of reminders

From the home screen of the Reminders app, tap **Edit** in the top corner then hit **Add Group**. Give the group a name then tap **Create**. You can now drag and drop reminders into this group to categorise them.

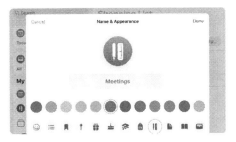

Assign a colour and icon

From the home screen of the Reminders app, slide a reminder towards the left then tap the **info** button. In the pop-up window, you'll be able to re-name the reminder, assign a colour and give it a unique icon.

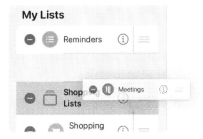

Delete reminders

From the home screen of the Reminders app, slide a reminder towards the left then tap the red **trash** icon to delete it. You can delete multiple lists and reminders by tapping **Edit** in the top-right corner.

Create a reminder using Siri

You can also add reminders by using Siri. Just hold the **Power** button, then say something like "*Remind me to pick up Sam*". Siri will then automatically create a new reminder.

Manage your Files

Discover how to manage files stored on your iPad and in Cloud...

If you've ever used a desktop computer or laptop, then you'll feel at home using the Files app. It's basically a Finder app for the iPad, letting you organise, edit, and delete files across all of your Apple devices and cloud services.

Open the Files app and you'll see the Browse screen, with shortcuts to search through your files, browse iCloud Drive, see local files on your iPad, and access any cloud-based services you have, such as Dropbox.

Files open or work in different ways depending on their file type. For example, images can be previewed, edited and marked up from within the Files app, while zip files can be previewed, but you can't extract their contents.

The basics

1 You can minimise the sidebar at any time by tapping this button.

2 Tap the **options** button in the sidebar to scan a document, connect to a server, or edit the sidebar contents.

3 Tap the **Icons** button in the top-right corner to change the view layout of a folder.

4 Search for a file on your iPad or within iCloud using this search field.

5 Tap and hold on a folder or file to copy, duplicate, rename, move, or delete it.

Swap to List or Icon view

If you want to fit more things onto the screen, tap the **Icons** button in the upper-right corner of the screen, then choose **List**.

Sort by size, date and name

Similarly, you can also use the **Icons** button to sort your files by name, date, size, or tag colour.

Tap and hold for more options

You can **tap and hold** on both folders and files to copy/duplicate/delete them, see more info, add a tag, favourite them and even compress/uncompress them.

See file information

If you want to see information about a file, such as its modified date or size and file type, **tap and hold** on the file until it lifts off the screen, let go then tap **Get Info** in the pop-up window.

Create a folder

Creating a new folder to organise your files is easy, just pull the window down, then tap the **New Folder** button in the upper-left corner.

Move a file into a folder

Tap the **Select** button at the top of the screen, select the file/s that you want to move, then tap **Move** at the bottom of the screen. You can then choose a new destination for the file.

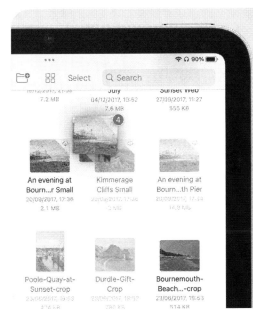

Drag and drop

One of the best features of the Files app is the ability to drag and drop files and folders. It makes organising your files a breeze, lets you move multiple files at once, and tag files using a swipe. To get started, **tap and hold** on a file until it attaches to your finger. You can drag this file to another location, into a folder, or slide it over a coloured tag.

You can also drag multiple files at once using Multi-Touch. To do this, **tap and hold on the first file**, then use one of your other fingers to tap on another file. You'll see it attach to the stack under your finger. You can keep doing this to add as many files as you like, then drag them to where they need to be and let go.

Select & Translate Live Text

Copy text from a photo, or translate text between languages...

There is so much useful information in your photos, from memorable places you've visited to handwritten family recipes. Your iPad uses secure on-device intelligence to help you discover more in your photos, quickly find what you're looking for and relive special moments.

One of the best ways it does this is via a feature called Live Text. It works by enabling you to open a photo on your iPad then select any text within the image; even if it's handwritten or hard to read. This means you can use familiar gestures to highlight, copy and paste text, and even translate it from one language to another. Live Text works in the Photos app, Camera, Screenshot, Quick Look and Safari.

Select text in a photo

If there is eligible text within a photo in your library, then it's possible to interact with this text in a number of ways. To see this in action, open an image in the Photos app that contains text. If your iPad recognises the text, it will show a Live Text button in the lower-right corner. Tap on this, and your iPad will highlight any text that you can interact with.

To select text, tap and hold on the highlighted area, then use the blue controls to select the precise words you need.

To find out more about text in an image, highlight it and then choose **Look Up**.

If there's a phone number in an image, tap the **Live Text** button in the lower-right corner. You'll then see options to:
- Call the number via your iPhone.
- Send a message to it.
- Make a FaceTime audio or video call.
- Add the number to your contacts.
- Copy the number.

Live Text also works in the Camera app, so you can open the Camera, point it at text or a number, and then interact with it son the spot.

Translate text

Live Text understands seven different languages: English, Chinese, French, Italian, German, Portuguese and Spanish. This means you can take a photo of a menu while abroad, and instantly translate it to English on the spot. As with Live Text, this feature works in both the Camera and Photos app. Here's how to use the translate feature:

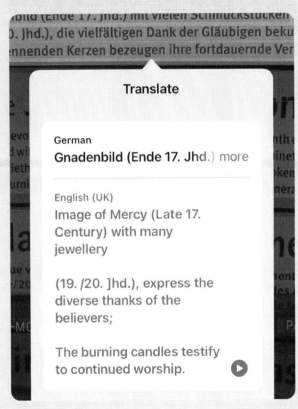

1 Open a photo or the Camera

Start by opening the Camera app, or by opening an image in the Photos app. Your iPad will automatically recognise any text and highlight it with a yellow box.

2 Highlight the text

Tap on the yellow box and the highlighted text will appear to hover above the image. Next, tap the **Translate** option.

3 See the translated text

A translate panel will slide up the screen. The original text will appear towards the top, with the translated text below. Below the text are the following options:

- Tap the **play** button to hear the text spoken out loud.

- Tap **Copy Translation** to copy the text to the clipboard.

- Tap **Change Language** to translate the original text to another language.

- Tap **Add to Favourites** to add the translation to the Translate app.

- Similarly, tap **Open in Translate** to view the text in the Translate app.

An overview of the Settings app

Get to know the basics of Settings...

Whenever you want to make a change to your iPad, adjust a setting, or update the operating system, then the Settings app is the place to go.

You can easily find the Settings app by looking for the icon with a cog gear in the centre:

Open the Settings app and you'll see a list of shortcuts to all the important settings on your iPad. They're labelled logically, so if you want to adjust how apps notify you, then tap on the Notifications shortcut. Similarly, if you want to connect to a new Wi-Fi network, tap Wi-Fi.

The basics

1 Search for individual settings using the search bar. If you don't see it, then pull the sidebar downwards using your finger.

2 Tap on your profile to access your Apple ID, where you can modify iCloud, iTunes, and device settings.

3 Enable Airplane mode from here if you're boarding an aircraft, or need to save battery.

4 Configure notifications from this shortcut. Other shortcuts from the Settings home screen include accessibility settings, Siri settings, and more.

5 Scroll the sidebar downwards to access additional settings, including individual app settings.

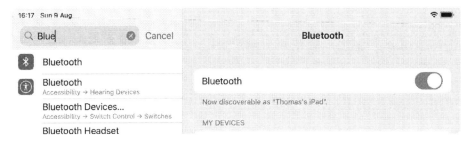

Search through Settings

The Settings app is packed with toggle switches, fields, and features for customising how your iPad works. Many are hidden away in sub-sections that you probably wouldn't find unless you were really determined, so if you need to quickly change a setting, open the **Settings** app and drag the sidebar down. A search bar will appear, enabling you to quickly find a setting or switch.

Find individual app settings

To access individual app settings, open **Settings** then scroll down. Keep going and you'll find individual app settings. You can also search for an app by using the search box.

Prevent apps from running in the background

If you're worried that an app is running in the background and using up battery, go to its Settings panel, then toggle **Background App Refresh** off.

Prevent an app from tracking your location

From the same Settings panel, you can also prevent an app from tracking your location. You can choose to let an app track you all the time, when it's open, or never.

Delete all of your data

If you're selling your iPad and want to wipe your data from it, go to **Settings > General > Transfer or Reset iPad**, then choose **Erase All Content and Settings**.

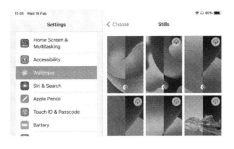

Choose a new wallpaper

Changing the background wallpaper is always a great way to freshen the look and feel of your device. It's easy to do, just open the **Settings** app, tap **Wallpaper,** then **Choose a New Wallpaper**.

Check for system updates

If you want to see if a new update is available for your iPad then go to **Settings > General > Software Update**. On the following panel you can download and install updates, or toggle Automatic Updates on.

Update your Apple ID

Open the **Settings** app and tap on your **profile photo** to update and access all of your Apple ID settings. You can also manage your other devices and subscriptions from here.

Use Screen Time to set limits

See how long you've spent using your iPad, and limit distractions...

If you're concerned or worried that you might be spending too long using your iPad, then the Screen Time panel included in the Settings app will help you work out exactly how long you've spent using apps, how many notifications you've received, or set time limits to prevent future distractions.

Find Screen Time

1 Open the **Settings** app, then tap on **Screen Time**.

2 Tap **See All Activity** at the top of the panel.

3 You can then view your Screen Time data for the current day or the last seven days.

As you'll see, the Screen Time panel is dense with information. You'll see total time spent with apps (some will be grouped into categories, such as "Productivity"), how many times you've picked up your iPad, and how many notifications you've received.

Downtime

Using the Screen Time settings panel it's possible to limit apps and notifications at a specific time, such as bedtime.

Set a Downtime schedule

Open the **Settings** app, tap on **Screen Time**, then choose **Downtime**. Toggle Downtime **on**, then use the **From** and **To** buttons to set a schedule.

Block inappropriate content

If you would like to limit inappropriate content, such as R-rated films or adult websites, tap on **Content & Privacy Restrictions**, then toggle it on. On the following screen you'll find a massive number of restriction options.

View an activity report of your iPad usage

Using the Screen Time panel it's possible to view daily or weekly reports of your iPad usage. You can see how long you've spent using apps, how many notifications you've received, and even how many times you've picked up your iPad.

1 Open the **Settings** app, then tap on **Screen Time.** At the top of the panel you should see a brief report on your iPad usage. Tap **See All Activity** to see more...

2 On the following panel you'll see a brief overview of the total time spent on your device, broken down into categories.

3 Beneath is a panel called Most Used. It displays which apps you've used the most during the day or last week. Tap on an app to see a detailed breakdown.

4 Below the Most Used panel is the Pickups panel. It displays exactly how many times you've picked up your iPad, as well as the average amount of time passed between each pickup.

5 Further below is report panel of the notifications you've received. It's broken down by app, so you can see exactly which app is sending you the most notifications.

Other things you can restrict using Screen Time

By visiting the **Content & Privacy** panel in the Screen Time settings, you can limit a massive amount of content and features on a device, including:

- App installation
- Location Sharing
- Changes to passcodes
- Account changes
- Mobile data limits

- Volume limit
- Explicit language
- Screen recording
- Multiplayer games
- Explicit entertainment and books

See which apps are draining battery

Losing battery quickly? Here's how to see which apps are responsible...

The battery inside your iPad is massive, taking up most of its inside and being responsible for most of its weight. You'll typically get a days usage out of your iPad, but if you've noticed that the battery is draining quickly, then it's possible to see which apps are responsible. You can also work out how long you've spent using your iPad, and how long it has been asleep.

Take a glance at your battery

If you're worried that an app or service is using all your battery, then you can access a time chart which displays the battery level and activity over the last 24 hours, or 10 days. To do this:

1 Open the **Settings** app, then tap on **Battery**.

2 Scroll down and you'll find two charts covering your battery's charge level and activity.

3 You can toggle between the last 24 hours or 10 days using the tab buttons above the charts.

4 Scroll down and you'll see a breakdown of which apps have used the most battery. Tap on one and you'll see the exact amount of time each app was used, and for how long it has been running in the background.

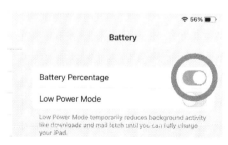

Show Battery Percentage

If your iPad is a little old and not lasting as long as it used to, go to **Settings** > **Battery**, then toggle **Battery Percentage** on. You'll now get a better idea of much battery power you have left.

View battery usage by app

Scroll down slightly and you'll see a list of all the apps you've used, and how much battery they've used up.

View app usage

Tap on the **SHOW ACTIVITY** button and you'll see how many minutes you've spent using each app.

Audio settings

Personalise your iPad to sound a little different...

A little personalisation can go a long way towards making your iPad feel like your own device. One of the easiest ways to do this is to alter the sound effects it emits. These include ringtones, email tones, tweet sound effects, calendar alerts, the lock sound, and keyboard clicks.

On this page, you'll learn how easy it is to select different tones and switch off sound effects that you might not need. You'll also discover how to set an automatic sound check feature, and set a volume limit.

Disable/enable Lock Sounds

You can disable or enable the lock sound effect by going to **Settings > Sounds**, then toggling the **Lock Sounds** switch near the bottom of the screen.

Change a text or ringtone alert

The buttons just below the volume slider enable you to choose from a wide variety of alert effects. Choose an option (such as **Text Tone**), then tap on a sound effect to preview and select it.

Download new tones

While selecting a new sound effect tone, tap the **Store** button to find new tones in the iTunes Store. Some are taken from popular music tracks, while others are custom sound effects purpose-built for your iPad.

Protect your hearing

To prevent hearing damage while using headphones, go to **Settings > Sounds**, then tap the **Reduce Lound Sounds** button. On the following screen, you can set a maximum decibel limit, with 85 decibels being the recommended amount.

Enable Sound Check

This clever feature will automatically scan your music files, then set an automatic level that lowers and increases the volume to make tracks and albums sound more coherent across the board. To enable it go to **Settings > Music**, then toggle the **Sound Check** switch on.

Turn off keyboard clicks

Your iPad will automatically emit a keyboard click sound every time you press a key on the on-screen keyboard. You can disable this by toggling the **Keyboard Clicks** switch at the bottom of the screen.

Customise the Pointer

Make it easier to see the pointer, or adjust its scrolling speed...

If you're using a Magic Mouse, Magic Keyboard or Trackpad to control your iPad, then it's possible adjust how quickly the pointer moves across the screen, its size, and even it's overall contrast.

Adjust mouse scrolling speed

Open the **Settings** app, tap on **Accessibility**, then choose **Pointer Control**. Look for the **Scrolling Speed** slider, then adjust it to either increase or decrease the movement sensitivity.

Adjust the pointer size

To make the pointer circle larger or smaller, go to **Settings > Accessibility > Pointer Control**, then adjust the **Pointer Size** slider.

Increase the pointer contrast

If you're struggling to see the pointer as it moves across the screen, go to **Settings > Accessibility > Pointer Control**, then toggle **Increase Contrast** on.

Change the pointer colour

It's possible to swap the default grey pointer to either blue, white, red, green, yellow or orange accents. To do this, go to **Settings > Accessibility > Pointer Control**, then tap the **Colour** option.

Adjust the auto-hide feature

By default, the pointer will hide two seconds after it has moved. You can toggle this on or off by going to **Settings > Accessibility > Pointer Control**, then toggle **Automatically Hide Pointer** off.

Disable pointer animations

With Pointer Animations enabled, the pointer morphs to match the shape of a hovered element, such as a button or app icon. If you'd rather it stay as a circular icon, go to **Settings > Accessibility > Pointer Control**, then toggle **Pointer Animations** off.

Customise Trackpad controls

Add additional features to your trackpad such as Tap to Click...

When you're using a trackpad with the iPad, such as a Magic Trackpad or the Magic Keyboard, a new panel is available in the Settings app. To find it open the Settings app and go to **General > Trackpad**. Here are some of the settings you can customise to ensure the trackpad works best for you...

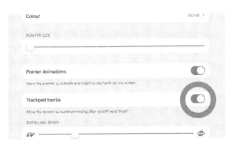

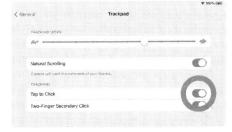

Turn off inertia animations

By default, the pointer will slide to a halt, rather than stop abruptly, if you quickly lift your finger while scrolling. To disable this, go to **Settings > Accessibility > Pointer Control**, then toggle **Trackpad Inertia** off.

Adjust scrolling speed

If you'd like to adjust the speed of the pointer when using a trackpad, go to **Settings > General > Trackpad**, then look for the **Tracking Speed** slider.

Enable Tap to Click

By enabling Tap to Click, it's possible to click on something by lightly tapping the trackpad with your finger. You'll find the Tap to Click option at **Settings > General > Trackpad**.

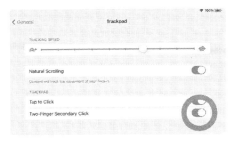

Two-Finger Secondary Click

Toggle **Two-Finger Secondary Click** on, and you can easily initiate the long-press feature found throughout iPadOS by tapping with two fingers.

Find out more about a Mouse or Trackpad

Turn to page **63** to find out more about using a mouse or trackpad with your iPad.

How to use Do Not Disturb

Prevent or limit interruptions...

It can be rather annoying when a message, FaceTime call, or notification awakes you at night, or when your iPad lights up and emits a noise during an important meeting. These notifications can usually be overridden by simply muting your device or putting it into Airplane mode, but the Do Not Disturb feature is simpler and much more effective.

It works by completely silencing your iPad between a determined period of time, for example, midnight and 7 AM. During this time, your iPad won't make a noise or light up. You can, however, tell it to allow notifications and repeat calls to come through from specific contacts.

Explore Do Not Disturb...

To activate or schedule Do Not Disturb, go to **Settings > Focus > Do Not Disturb**, then toggle it **on**. You can then...

- **Schedule Do Not Disturb.** Look for TURN ON AUTOMATICALLY , tap on it, then toggle **Schedule** on. You can now use the **From** and **To** buttons to set a schedule.

- **Set an automation.** You can tell Do Not Disturb to automatically activate at a specific time, at a location, or when you open an app. To do this, look towards the bottom of the Do Not Disturb panel, then tap **Add Schedule or Automation**. On the following screen you can use the three options to make your choice.

Enable Do Not Disturb

Swipe down from the top-right corner of the screen to access Control Centre, tap on **Focus**, then tap **Do Not Disturb**. This will instantly enable Do Not Disturb, preventing any calls, messages or notifications from alerting you.

Activate for a period of time

To quickly activate Do Not Disturb for the next hour, until the morning, or until you leave your current location, tap on the **options** button next to Do Not Disturb within Control Centre, then select an option.

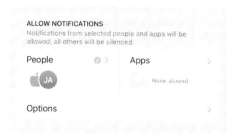

Let repeat calls through

To let specific people get in touch when Do Not Disturb is active, go to the **Do Not Disturb** panel and tap on the **People** option. On the following screen you can add people from your contacts book by tapping the **Add** button.

Siri settings

Adjust Siri's voice, language, and features...

Siri is a great digital assistant for asking questions, setting reminders, and sending messages, and it's highly customisable. By visiting the Siri & Search panel in the Settings app, you can change the voice and language, toggle "Hey Siri" on and off, announce messages out-loud and more.

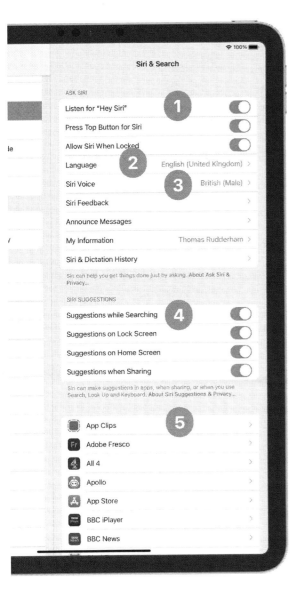

Explore Siri & Search...

You can find all the Siri settings by going to **Settings** > **Siri & Search**...

1. **Listen for "Hey Siri".** When this is toggled on, you can activate Siri by saying "Hey Siri" out-loud near your iPad.

2. **Language.** Tap this option to choose from 20 different languages. For example, you can swap between English (United Kingdom), English (New Zealand), and English (India).

3. **Siri Voice.** This option lets you choose between male and female voices or localised accents.

4. **Siri Suggestions.** As you use your iPad, Siri will try to learn your habits by monitoring which apps you use and how you search your device. You can toggle these features on or off using these switches.

5. **App Suggestions.** As above, over time Siri learns how you use and interact with apps. You can switch off this feature for individual apps by selecting an app, then toggling off the switch called **Learn from this App**.

A guide to accessibility settings

Enable visual, audio, and physical accommodations...

Your iPad might be an intuitive device to use, but it's also packed with assistive features to help those with visual impairments or motor control limitations. You'll find the majority of them in the Accessibility panel within the Settings app. To get there, open **Settings**, tap **General**, then select **Accessibility**.

Invert the colours

To flip the colours of your iPad's screen, go to **Settings > Accessibility > Display & Text Size**. You'll see two options: Smart Invert, and Classic Invert. Smart Invert will reverse the colour of everything except images, media and a limited number of apps. Classic Invert will reverse the colour of everything on the screen.

Enable button shapes

Buttons in iOS usually look like a word or short piece of text. To make it more obvious which is a button and which is a piece of information, go to **Settings > Accessibility > Display & Text Size**, then toggle the **Button Shapes** switch **on**. This will display thin blue lines beneath buttons, and add small radio buttons to the inside of toggle switches.

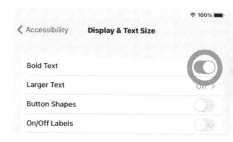

Bold text

A handy accessibility feature for those with vision impairments is the Bold Text toggle switch. Once activated, it makes text on the display appear to be bolder. To turn on Bold Text, go to **Settings > Accessibility > Display & Text Size**, then toggle **Bold Text on**.

Show subtitles and captions

To enable subtitles and captions for entertainment on your iPad, go to **Settings > Accessibility > Subtitles & Captioning**, and toggle the top switch **on**.

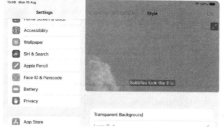

Style subtitles and captions

After enabling subtitles, tap the **Style** button to choose from three preset styles. By tapping **Create New Style** you can customise the font, size, colour, and background style.

Use slow keys to help you type

If it takes a while for you to type individual keys, then go to **Settings > Accessibility > Keyboards > Slow Keys**, and toggle it on. You can now adjust how long you have to press a key before it is activated.

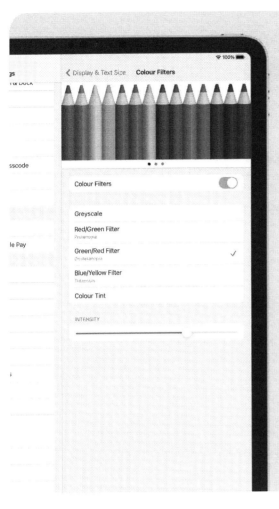

Adjust the display to accommodate for colour blindness

Colour blindness can be a hassle at the best of times in the real world, and it's a problem that remains when using your iPad to browse the web, examine photographs or generally interact with the user interface.

Thankfully a built-in accessibility feature can adjust the colour palette of the display to accommodate for colour blindness, making it possible to see tricky colours in a wide range of spectrums. Here's how it works:

1. Open the **Settings** app and go to **Accessibility > Display & Text Size > Colour Filters** then toggle **Colour Filters** on.

2. You'll see a preview of the effect in the graphic at the top of the screen (scroll it left to see two colour charts).

3. To fine tune the colour spectrum change, tap the filters below the image.

Connect a hearing aid to your iPad

By connecting a hearing aid to your iPad you can experience higher-quality FaceTime calls. Go to **Settings > Accessibility > Hearing Devices**, where you can connect to any Bluetooth-enabled hearing aids. Any hearing aids with HAC compatibility (visit support.apple.com/kb/HT4526 to see a list of compatible devices) will also enable you to increase and decrease the volume independently for both ears, monitor battery usage and more.

Change the audio balance

If you're hard of hearing in one ear, or have a faulty pair of headphones, then it's possible to adjust the volume level in either the left or right channels. Go to **Settings > Accessibility > Audio/Visual**, then look for a slider with L on the left side, and R on the right. Drag it left or right to adjust the volume. It might help to play music via the Music app while you make the adjustment.

L   R

Assistive Touch

Assistive Touch is a helpful feature for those with impaired physical and motor skills. It enables you to activate Multi-Touch features such as pinch-to-zoom with only one finger, or to trigger hardware buttons. To enable Assistive Touch, go to **Settings > Accessibility > Touch > Assistive Touch**, then toggle the button at the top of the screen.

With Assistive Touch enabled, you'll see a small square button appear on the side of the screen. By tapping this you can access a series of shortcut buttons which enable you to activate Notification Centre, Control Centre, Siri, functions on your iPad, return to the Home screen, or quickly access your favourite gestures.

Create an Assistive Touch gesture

If you'd like to mimic a Multi-Touch gesture (such as zoom) using Assistive Touch, then it's possible to do this by using a custom gesture. To create one, go to the Assistive Touch panel in the Settings app, then tap the **Create New Gesture** button. On the following screen, use two fingers to mimic zooming out of an image. Once you've done, tap **Save**. You can now use this gesture from the Assistive Touch panel by tapping the **Custom** button, indicated by a star.

Ask your iPad to read out-loud

Siri is great for setting reminders, opening apps, or finding out what's on at the cinema, but you can also use Siri to read out loud selected text, messages, and notes. This feature, called Speak Selection, is particularly useful for those with impaired eyesight.

To turn on Speak Selection go to **Settings > Accessibility > Spoken Content**, then toggle **Speak Selection**.

To speak words out loud, highlight any text (by double tapping or tapping and holding on it), then tap the **Speak** button in the pop-up menu.

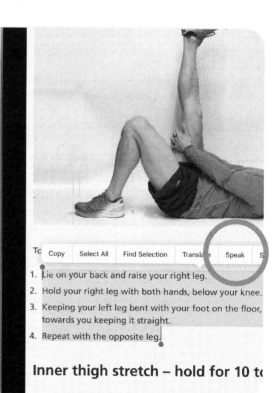

1. Lie on your back and raise your right leg.
2. Hold your right leg with both hands, below your knee.
3. Keeping your left leg bent with your foot on the floor, towards you keeping it straight.
4. Repeat with the opposite leg.

Inner thigh stretch – hold for 10 to

Change the voice accent

From the **Spoken Content** panel (see previous tip), tap the **Voices** link and you can choose from a wide range of voices from the Speech menu. These include Australian accents, British accents, Spanish, Hindi and much more.

Speak Screen

This helpful feature works by reading out-loud all the content that's currently on-screen. To enable Speak Screen, toggle its switch on from the **Speech** panel, then whenever you want to hear what's on-screen, swipe down from the top of the screen with two fingers. A panel will appear that enables you to control speech playback. To close the panel, simply tap the **X** button.

Highlight words

Notice the **Highlight Content** button? Toggle this switch to see the words highlighted as your iPad reads them out-loud. Think of Karaoke and you'll get an idea of how this works.

Use a magnifying glass

The iPad is designed to be easy for anyone to use, even those with visual impairments. However, there might be occasions where you need to zoom into the screen. Those with visual impairments might also appreciate the ability to get a closer look at things on the screen. Using a three-fingered Multi-Touch gesture, it's possible to display an on-screen magnifying glass, which you can move around to examine things in more detail. Here's how it works:

1. Go to **Settings > Accessibility**, then tap the **Zoom** option near the top of the screen.

2. You'll see a magnifying glass appear on-screen.

3. You can move the magnifying glass around by dragging the small button at the bottom of it.

4. You can hide the magnifying glass by tapping twice on the screen with three fingers.

Index

Quickly find what you're looking for...

Stay inspired

Other Ultimate Guides:

iPad Pro: Ultimate Guide

978-1-914347-05-4

$19.75 USA
$22.99 CAN
£10.99 UK
$22.99 AUD

Mac: Ultimate Guide

978-1-914347-08-5

$19.75 USA
$22.99 CAN
£10.99 UK
$22.99 AUD

iPhone: Ultimate Guide

978-1-914347-06-1

$19.75 USA
$22.99 CAN
£10.99 UK
$22.99 AUD

Android: Ultimate Guide

978-1-914347-85-6

$19.75 USA
$22.99 CAN
£10.99 UK
$22.99 AUD

Windows: Ultimate Guide

978-1-914347-84-9

$19.75 USA
$22.99 CAN
£10.99 UK
$22.99 AUD

Information & History:

Formula One: The Illustrated History

978-1-914347-88-7

$18.99 USA
$25.99 CAN
£9.99 UK
$22.99 AUD

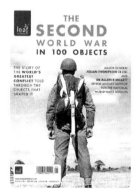

Second World War in 100 Objects

978-1-914347-89-4

$18.99 USA
$25.99 CAN
£9.99 UK
$22.99 AUD

Beatles Album by Album

978-1-914347-91-7

$18.99 USA
$25.99 CAN
£9.99 UK
$22.99 AUD

Visit www.leafpublishing.co.uk to find out more

Printed in Great Britain
by Amazon

29325469R00082